I
TALK
BACK
TO THE
DEVIL

I TALK BACK TO THE DEVIL

essays in spiritual perfection

A.W. TOZER
Edited by
Gerald B. Smith

Also published in cloth binding as
Volume Four of The Tozer Pulpit Series

christian publications, inc.
25 South Tenth Street, Harrisburg, Pa. 17101

The Mark of *CP* Vibrant Faith

Contents

Preface

In his lifetime, Dr. A. W. Tozer was quick to admit that he could take no delight in preaching on spiritual perfection themes, because of the reality of meeting Satan's opposition head-on.

When preaching the twelve sermons which are published here, Pastor Tozer told his Chicago congregation:

"I have never given more time and more pain and more prayer to any other series of sermons in my ministry.

"Because of their importance, I have literally felt Satan attempting to thwart the purpose of God. I have felt I was in raw contact with hell.

"There are so many in the Church who are spiritually blind that I tell God that I want to be able to see—I want to be a lower-case 'seer.' I want to penetrate and understand and have discernment concerning the whole plan of God. I want to appraise the situation and see it as God sees it—to know the role of God in this day of religious confusion.

"Now, that doesn't make a man easy to live with. It doesn't make him popular and it doesn't create any problem for police taking care of the crowd.

"This course has forced me frequently to follow the trail of opposition and temptation straight to the foe! But I would rather have it this way than to have to admit—as some will have to admit—to having spent a lifetime preaching the Word of God and yet never having met the devil once in open combat!

"In my preparation, there have been struggles and combat, moans and pains. I think this is the conflict of Jesus being re-lived in His people. And some of you have felt it, too. Some of you have come out into a newer, more blessed and happier experience in God, which is only beginning for you!

"I have received mail concerning these sermons. The courageous ones signed. The cowards wrote without signing their names. Their suggestion seems to be that I am a 'show-off' to preach about perfection, and that I am trying to get a reputation for being 'saintly.'

"But, I will tell you something—it is a delightful thing when you know that you are close enough to the adversary that you can hear him roar! Too many Christians never get into 'lion country' at all!"

Most of you who will now go on to read Dr. Tozer's straight-forward appeals for Christ-like living did not hear the sermons as they were preached. So, it is our hope—as it was Dr. Tozer's for his hearers—that you will resist the temptations to become a "run-of-the-mill" Christian and that you will press on into blessed victory in "lion country"!

Chapter One

I Talk Back
to the Devil!

"The devil makes it his business to keep Christians in bondage, bound and gagged, actually imprisoned in their own grave clothes!"

Why doesn't the old devil, Satan, give up and bow out of the picture when a person becomes a believing Christian?

Although he is a dark and sinister foe dedicated to the damnation of humans, I think he knows that it is no use trying to damn a forgiven and justified child of God who is in the Lord's hands.

So, it becomes the devil's business to keep the

9

Christian's spirit imprisoned. He knows that the believing and justified Christian has been raised up out of the grave of his sins and trespasses. From that point on, Satan works that much harder to keep us bound and gagged, actually imprisoned in our own grave clothes.

He knows that if we continue in this kind of bondage, we will never be able to claim our rightful spiritual heritage. He knows also that while we continue bound in this kind of enslavement we are not much better off than when we were spiritually dead.

This is one reason why the Christians in today's churches are behaving like a flock of frightened sheep—so intimidated by the devil that we can't even say "Amen!"

I admit that occasionally you find a few who are just childishly happy about everything, but that is not what I mean. Often these are just like children playing in the market places, having never been seriously engaged in the conflict on the spiritual battlefield.

Show me an individual or a congregation committed to spiritual progress with the Lord, interested in what the Bible teaches about spiritual perfection and victory, and I will show you where there is strong and immediate defiance by the devil!

Satan has been in this business of intimidating and silencing and oppressing the people of God for a long, long time.

The armies of Israel experienced this kind of fright in the valley of Elah when Goliath with the Philistines were camped on the opposite mountain. King Saul was leading Israel, but he was sour, fearful, intimidated because of Goliath, that giant of a man who daily shouted his taunts, "I defy the army of Israel this day!" So the army cowered in fear.

But a little fellow by the name of David came along, and he was in right fellowship with the Lord. We are told that the spirit of the Lord came upon David, who said to the Israelites, "Let no man's heart fail—thy servant will go and fight with this Philistine!"

This was the first word of encouragement to come to these ranks of soldiers who had been able only to gaze in fascinated fear at that great giant who taunted them daily. David was confident and serene because he knew and trusted the Source of all strength. The recorded result was one of the great, miraculous "turn-arounds" of history, David and his sling disposing of Goliath in a way that brought glory to the God of Israel as well as victory to the armies of Israel.

I am sure that it is not glorifying to our God that Christians should be so intimidated and silenced in our day. It was Jesus Christ, the Lord of glory, who came down and took our human body for Himself. He was a man, born of a woman, a man wearing our own nature—but He was also God!

He went out to the cross and they sacrificed Him there. The Father, God Almighty, accepted His sacrifice as the one, last, final fulfillment and consummation of all the sacrifices ever made on Jewish altars. After He had been dead three days, He came forth—raised from the dead and out of the grave. After a few days He ascended as Victor over all the forces of death and hell and sat down amid the acclamations of the heavenly hosts!

There He sits at God's right hand—a living man, our representative and advocate and great high

11

priest. Believing this, we ought to be the most fearless, the most relaxed, the happiest and most God-assured people in the whole world!

But Satan is an old dragon who defies us to this hour. He is saying to Christians, "I defy you—what can you do about it?"

I think we had better get free! We must face up to the issues and attitudes and doubts which constitute our fears, that keep us from being happy and victorious Christians with the true liberty of the children of God. We seem to quake about many things.

In the first place, are you still afraid of your past sins? God knows that sin is a terrible thing—and the devil knows it, too. So he follows us around and as long as we will permit it, he will taunt us about our past sins.

As for myself, I have learned to talk back to him on this score. I say, "Yes, Devil, sin is terrible—but I remind you that I got it from you! And I remind you, Devil, that everything good—forgiveness and cleansing and blessing—everything that is good I have freely received from Jesus Christ!"

Everything that is bad and that is against me I got from the devil—so why should he have the effrontery and the brass to argue with me about it? Yet he will do it because he is the devil, and he is committed to keeping God's children shut up in a little cage, their wings clipped so that they can never fly!

In our churches we often sing, "Arise, my soul, arise; shake off thy guilty fears." But nothing happens and we keep our fears. Why do we claim on one hand that our sins are gone and on the other act just as though they are not gone?

Brethren, we have been declared "Not Guilty!" by the highest court in all the universe. Still there are honest Christians, earnestly seeking the face of God, who cannot seem to break loose and find real freedom. The grave clothes trip them up every time they try to move on a little faster. Satan uses their past sins to terrify them.

Now, on the basis of grace as taught in the Word of God, when God forgives a man, He trusts him as though he had never sinned. God did not have mental reservations about any of us when we became His children by faith. When God forgives a man, He doesn't think, "I will have to watch this fellow because he has a bad record." No, He starts with him again as though he had just been created and as if there had been no past at all! That is the basis of our Christian assurance—and God wants us to be happy in it.

Next, are you allowing Satan to magnify the memories of your spiritual failures? He will always keep them before you unless you take your stand and move up in faith.

The devil will whisper, "You didn't get very far along toward the deeper life, did you?"

He will say, "You made a big 'to-do' about wanting to be filled with the Spirit and you really flopped, didn't you?"

He will taunt you with the fact that you may have stumbled in the faith—and perhaps more than once! The devil wants you to live in a state of discouraged chagrin and remorse.

Remember, the Bible does not teach that if a man falls down, he can never rise again. The fact that he falls is not the most important thing—but rather that he is forgiven and allows God to lift him up!

Perhaps you have read of the saintly Fletcher, whose holy life became so recognized that he was

13

called "the seraphic Fletcher." His testimony reveals that he stumbled and miserably failed God seven times. But after the seventh failure he went to a room and did not come out until he was able to rest his case completely in the strength of God's hands. He came out of the room saying, "Dear Lord, I believe that I am delivered from the bondage of my sin. If you will keep me and help me I will never cease telling the world what you can do for a man!" For the rest of his life Fletcher exhibited to the world God's power to bless and to keep His transformed children on earth.

If our failures are going to hinder us forever, we might just as well never have taken the first step. But God knew all about us and He still loved us and desired His eternal best for us.

The Bible tells us often that God knows humans better than they know themselves—He doesn't have to wait for the information to come from the accuser, the devil.

God has said, "I knew that you would deal very treacherously and that you were called a transgressor from the womb; but for my name's sake I will defer my anger and for my praise I will refrain that I cut thee not off. Behold, I have refined thee but not with silver, I have chosen thee in the furnace of affliction. For mine own sake, even mine own sake, will I do it."

God does have a stake in each of us—and it is for His own sake that He will lift us up. He is not going to bless us for our own sake—He is going to bless us for Jesus' sake and for the sake of His own name!

If you think that there is anyone in the world so good that God could do something for that person's sake, you don't know sin; and if you think there is anything that God will not do for you for His sake and for His name, you don't know God!

If you have failed, remember that you are not responsible to men in this regard. You stand responsible before your heavenly Father and Jesus Christ at the right hand of God. Let us be encouraged by this good news!

In the third place, some are fearful that they will lose their reputation as sober and conservative and traditional Christians. In other words, they have never been willing to be a fool for Jesus' sake!

It is amazing that genuine Christians are not willing to stand up wherever they are and give a good word for the Lord. There are great political ideologies sweeping the world now whose members will make double-eyed, long-eared donkeys of themselves for the sake of the party and the cause. There are religious sects whose witnesses are willing to go to jail, to be pushed around, to be lampooned for the sake of a miserable, twisted doctrine! But in our Christian ranks, we prefer to be respectable and smooth, and we have a reputation for being very solemn Christian believers.

I can only conclude from my experience that many solemn, professing Christians will never make any spiritual progress and will never really be happy in the Lord until God finds some way to shake them out of their deadly respectability!

Charles G. Finney, the great American evangelist, knew this experience of becoming God's man and God's mouthpiece in such a way and with such unusual blessing and results that many just stood as critics and tried to frown him down.

So it has been with all of God's saints who have pleased Him and praised Him through the centuries. At some time in their witness and expression of

15

the living Christ they have had to lose their reputations among those who have been traditionally pious and somber, dogmatic and cautious.

This is still happening in our day, and with glorious results.

A young man who is director of one of our American Bible conferences has given me his testimony of great and radical things which the Lord has done for him in recent months.

"I realize now that in my service for God I was one of the most self-assured, conceited and horrid young fellows you could ever meet," he told me frankly. "I could raise money, I could put on a great program, and I figured I was a great success in the Lord's work.

"But recently on a trip to Wales, I had the opportunity of talking to some older folks who remembered Evan Roberts and the great Welsh revival. They told me about the true working of the Holy Spirit in Christian renewal and revival—and I didn't really know what they were talking about.

"Somehow, and they did not realize it, it was just as though they were burying me under a great load of crushing bricks, and God spoke to me about my own great spiritual lack."

He told me that he made his way to the little cottage where he was staying and got down on his knees and began to sweat it out before God.

Do you know what this was? It was the act of dying! It was the end of self. That man died to reputation, ability, presumption, success, conceit, personality—all of that stuff!

He said to me, "Mr. Tozer, I was filled with the Holy Spirit and my whole life has been transformed. Now I only want this cheated and betrayed generation to see the glory of God once more!"

I said to him then, "Brother, do you realize that if you carry through with this message and this blessing that you will lose some of your best fundamentalist friends? You will be described as having gone off your rocker."

"I am not worried any more about my reputation," he replied. "I am perfectly willing because I am going to let the Lord have His way in the whole operation."

The interesting thing is that he hasn't had to switch or change his doctrines around at all—he just found out that he needed the fire of God on his doctrine, and he got it!

Also related to reputation is the fear of many Christians that they will be considered fanatical or extreme for their Christian faith. I think it is ironical that the devil gives the world all of its extremists in every realm—entertainment, politics, society, education, anarchy, intrigue—you name it! Yet it is the same devil that frightens believers about the great danger of becoming "extreme."

I passed an auditorium recently where one of the young crowd of singing stars was appearing. Police were having great trouble with the crowds and in the erotic fury of that concert, girls began to tear off their clothes; many were weeping and screaming. Those who had fainted were being carried out.

It is the same devil, but he uses different tactics in dealing with Christians. Should a Christian get blessed and say, "Amen," the devil quickly intervenes and whispers, "Don't be a fanatic—you ought to stay quiet and stable in the faith!"

Oh, what a devil the devil is! He frightens us first and then sells us a bill of goods about caution, caution, caution in the church.

17

Some Christians also are greatly awed by the fear of ostracism. The devil says to them, "Be careful about religion—you will be lonely. You will have to go it alone!"

I have heard one of our preachers tell about the experience he had years ago in coming to a decision concerning the claims of Christ on his life. It was at the close of a service, and he was standing with the rest of the congregation while an invitation was being given to come forward in submission to the will of God. There was a struggle going on in his own soul, and he knew that the Spirit of God was pressing him to make the decision to sell out completely and to become a real Christian in commitment to the Lord.

But the devil knows how to join in these arguments, and he whispered, "Charlie, you must be careful at this point. You know how easy it would be to break up your marriage and break up your home. You know how staid and strait-laced and conservative your wife is about religion. Don't do anything that would break up your home, Charlie!"

But the Spirit of God persisted, and Charlie found himself answering the call. He went forward and knelt at the altar for heart-searching and prayer.

Suddenly he thought he heard someone weeping at his side. Then he was sure that it sounded like his wife. Turning, he found that it was his wife, for she had been just a few feet behind him when he made his way to the altar. Together they made their commitment to Christ and to His service.

For a long time, you see, Satan had been telling Charlie that his wife would never be willing to yield to joyful Christian dedication. But the devil is a liar and the father of lies! He never tells the truth

18

unless he can use it to whip you and embarrass you—unless he can use it in his attempts to ruin you and destroy you!

There also seems to be a chilling fear of holy enthusiasm among the people of God. We try to tell how happy we are—but we remain so well-controlled that there are very few waves of glory experienced in our midst.

Some of you go to the ball game and you come back whispering because you are hoarse from shouting and cheering. But no one in our day ever goes home from church with a voice hoarse from shouts brought about by a manifestation of the glory of God among us.

Actually our apathy about praise in worship is like an inward chill in our beings. We are under a shadow and we are still wearing the grave clothes. You can sense this in much of our singing in the contemporary church. Perhaps you will agree that in most cases it is a kind of plodding along, without the inward life of blessing and victory and resurrection joy and overcoming in Jesus' name.

Why is this? It is largely because we are looking at what we are, rather than responding to who Jesus Christ is! We have often failed and have not been overcomers because our trying and striving have been in our own strength. That leaves us very little to sing about!

Dr. A. B. Simpson wrote:

"Fainting soldier of the Lord,
Hear His sweet, inspiring word;
'I have conquered all thy foes,
I have suffered all thy woes.
Struggling soldier, trust in Me,
I have overcome for thee!' "

This has to be the secret of our praise and enthusiasm—Jesus Christ is our Overcomer! In our own strength we cannot overcome anyone or anything.

"Fear not though thy foes be strong,
Fear not though the strife be long;
Trust thy glorious Captain's power,
Watch with Him one little hour.
Hear Him calling, 'Follow Me,
I have overcome for thee!'"

Brethren, human activity and human sweat and tears work not the victory of Christ! It took the sweat and tears and blood of the Lord Jesus Christ. It took the painful dying and the victorious resurrection and ascension to bring us the victory!

It is for us to trust, to trust wholly in the Lord Jesus. This is the only way in which we can conquer fear and live in blessed victory.

I have had times in my life and ministry when the burdens and the pressures seemed to be too much. Sometimes physical weariness adds to our problems and our temptation to give in to discouragement and doubt. At these times it seems that even in prayer it is impossible to rise above the load. More than once, by faith that seemed to have been imparted directly from heaven, the Lord has enabled me to claim all that I needed for body, soul and spirit. On my knees I have been given freedom and strength to pray, "Now, Lord, I have had enough of this—I refuse to take any more of this heaviness and oppression! This does not come from God—this comes from my enemy, the devil! Lord, in Jesus' name, I will not take it any longer—through Jesus Christ I am victor!" At these times, great burdens have just melted and rolled away—all at once!

Brethren, God never meant for us to be kicked around like a football. He wants us to be humble and let Him do the chastening when necessary. But when the devil starts tampering with you, dare to resist him!

I stand for believing in God and defying the devil —and our God loves that kind of courage among His people.

If you are still wrapped in grave clothes and great fears lie upon you, it is time for you to dare to rise and in sweet faith in the risen Jesus Christ declare: "I will not take this any longer. I am a child of God—why should I go mourning all the day?"

Will God answer?

"All right, My child," He will answer as the burden rolls away, "I have waited long to hear you say that. Jesus is Victor and in Him you overcome!"

Chapter Two

Christianity—
Fun and Games?

"Certainly, not all of the mystery of the Godhead can be known by man. But, just as certainly, all that man can know of God in this life is revealed in Jesus Christ!"

Some Christian believers seemingly are committed to endless dialogue about the deeper life just as though it were some new kind of fun and games.

I almost shrink from hearing the expression, "the deeper life," because so many people want to talk about it as a topic—but no one seems to want to know and love God for Himself!

God is the deeper life! Jesus Christ Himself is

the deeper life, and as I plunge on into the knowledge of the triune God, my heart moves on into the blessedness of His fellowship. This means that there is less of me and more of God—thus my spiritual life deepens, and I am strengthened in the knowledge of His will.

I think this is what Paul meant when he penned that great desire, "That I may know Him!" He was expressing more than the desire for acquaintance—he was yearning to be drawn into the full knowledge of fellowship with God which has been provided in the plan of redemption.

God originally created man in His own image so that man could know companionship with God in a unique sense and to a degree which is impossible for any other creature to experience.

Because of his sin, man lost this knowledge, this daily partnership with God. In the first chapter of Romans, Paul gives us a vivid picture of men and women whom God gave over to a reprobate mind because they did not wish to retain God in their knowledge, their foolish hearts being darkened.

This is the Bible portrait of man. He has that great potential of knowing God as no other creature can, but he is lost; and without God in his knowledge, his conduct is unworthy of his high origin and his being despairs in its encompassing emptiness.

This despair, this emptiness and lostness, reflects man's great problem because he is an intelligent, moral creature who has left his proper sphere and estate of environment. How can he know anything but endless defeat and pain, because as a sinner he is not fulfilling the great end for which he was created?

We believe that God created all living creatures, each with its own peculiar kind of life. God adjusted that life in each case to its own environment. Therefore, as long as each living creature remains in its own environment and lives the kind of life for which it was created, it fulfills the purpose for which it was made. Thus, the highest that can be said of any creature is that it fulfilled the purpose for which God made it.

According to the scriptures, only man was created in God's own image. I can find no reference in the Bible to indicate that God made the seraphim or cherubim, angels or archangels in His own image.

I know that I take a chance of being misunderstood and perhaps of being misjudged when I state that man was more like God than any other creature ever created. Because of the nature of man's creation, there is nothing in the universe so much like God as the human soul. Even in the face of man's sin and lost condition, there is still that basic potential in the soul and nature of man that through grace can become more like God than anything in the universe.

There is no question about man's sin—therefore, there is no question about his being lost. A man is lost if he is not converted—overwhelmed in the vast darkness of emptiness. He was created to know God, but he chose the gutter. That is why he is like a bird shut away in a cage or like a fish taken from the water. That is the explanation of man's disgraceful acts—war and hate, murder and greed, brother against brother!

Once the smart men told us that science and philosophy and psychiatry and sociology would soon make the world a better place in which to live. As time passes, however, men are at one another's throats as never before and there is the greatest volume of hate, suspicion, anarchy, treachery, espionage, murder and criminal acts of all kinds in the history of the world.

Is there still a good word for man in his lost condition? Is there an answer for man in whom there is that instinctive groping and craving for the lost image and the knowledge of the Eternal Being?

Yes, there is a positive answer found in the Word of God, and it teaches the sinner-man that it is still possible for him to know God. The Bible teaches us that God has not abandoned the human race as He abandoned the angels who sinned and gave up their first estate.

Studying the Word of God, we must come to the conclusion that God abandoned the sinning angels because they had not been created in the image of God. They were moral creatures, capable of moral and spiritual perception, but they were not made in God's image.

And why has God given sinful man another opportunity in salvation through the merits of a Redeemer? Only because he was made in the image of God, and God has expressed His own everlasting love for man through the giving of His Son.

Now, the Bible has a great deal to say about the manner in which sinful man may come into the fellowship and the presence of God, and it all has to do with forgiveness and grace and regeneration and justification in Jesus Christ! It all boils down to the teaching that Jesus Christ is everything that the Godhead is! The image of the invisible God, the brightness of His glory, the express image of His person—all of these we find in and through Jesus Christ!

We believe with rejoicing that Jesus Christ was the begotten of the Father, before all ages, that He is God of God, Light of light, very God of very

God, begotten and not made, of one substance with the Father, and it is by Him that all things were made!

I advise you not to listen to those who spend their time demeaning the person of Christ. I advise you to look beyond the cloudiness of modern terms used by those who themselves are not sure who Jesus Christ was, in reality.

You cannot trust the man who can only say, "I believe that God revealed Himself through Christ." Find out what he really believes about the person of the incarnate Son of God!

You cannot trust the man who will only say that Christ reflected more of God than other men do. Neither can you trust those who teach that Jesus Christ was the supreme religious genius, having the ability to catch and reflect more of God than any other man.

All of these approaches are insults to the person of Jesus Christ. He was and is and can never cease to be God, and when we find Him and know Him, we are back at the ancient fountain again! Christ is all that the Godhead is!

This is the wonder, the great miracle—that by one swift, decisive, considered act of faith and prayer, our souls go back to the ancient fountain of our being, and we start over again! This means back beyond the angels, back beyond the beginning of the world, back beyond where Adam started—back to the glorious, flowing fountain we call the being of God, the Triune God!

It is in Jesus Christ Himself that we find our source, our satisfaction. I think this is what John Newton perceived in the miracle of the new birth, causing him to sing, "Now rest my long-divided heart, fixed on this blissful center—rest!"

Can there be any explanation for the fact that we seem to know so little of Jesus Christ even after He has made Himself and His blessings so readily available to His believing children?

Part of the answer may be found in our own human reasoning which becomes so easily discouraged in the face of God's infinity and God's character.

Brethren, it is well for us to remember that as human beings we can never know all of the Godhead. If we were capable of knowing all of the Godhead perfectly, we would be equal to the Godhead. For illustration, we know that we cannot pour an entire quart of water into a vessel which has a capacity of less than a quart. So, you could never pour all of the Godhead into the experience of any being who is less than God Himself.

A similar kind of illustration was used long ago by ancient fathers in the church as they argued for the trinity in the Godhead. They pointed out that God the eternal Father is an infinite God, and He is love. The very nature of love is to give itself but the Father could not give His love fully to anyone not fully equal to Himself. Thus we have the revelation of the Son Who is equal to the Father and of the eternal Father pouring out His love into the Son, Who could contain it, because the Son is equal with the Father. Further, these ancient wise men reasoned, if the Father were to pour out His love on the Son, a medium of communication equal both to the Father and to the Son would be required, and this was the Holy Ghost. So we have their concept of the Trinity—the ancient Father in the fullness of His love pouring Himself through the Holy Ghost, Who is in being equal to Him, into the Son Who is in being equal to the Spirit and to the Father.

Certainly not all of the mystery of the Godhead can be known by man, but just as certainly, all that man can know of God in this life is revealed in Jesus Christ. When the Apostle Paul said with yearning, "That I may know Him," he was not speaking of intellectual knowledge, that which can be learned and memorized, but Paul was speaking of the reality of an experience, that of knowing God personally and consciously, spirit touching spirit and heart touching heart.

There are many in the churches of our day who talk some of the Christian language but who know God only by hearsay. Most of them have read some book about God. They have seen some reflection of the light of God. They may have heard some faint echo of the voice of God, but their own personal knowledge of God is very slight.

Many Christians are staking their reputations on church attendance, religious activity, social fellowship, sessions of singing—because in all of these things they are able to lean on one another. They spend a lot of time serving as religious props for one another in Christian circles.

When Jesus was here upon the earth, the record shows that He had work to do and He also knew the necessity for activity as He preached and healed, taught and answered questions and blessed the people. He also knew the fellowship of His brethren, those who followed Him and loved Him. But these were the incidental things in Jesus' life compared to His fellowship with and personal knowledge of the Father. When Jesus went into the mountain to pray and wait on God all night, He was not alone, for He knew the conscious presence of the Father with Him.

In our modern Christian service we are constantly pressed to do this and to do that, and to go here and go there. How often we miss completely the conscious presence of God with the result that we know God only by hearsay!

Again, part of the answer we are looking for is the fact that so many professing Christians just want to get things from God. Anyone can write a book now that will sell—just give it a title like, *Seventeen Ways to Get Things from God!* You will have immediate sales. Or, write a book called, *Fourteen Ways to Have Peace of Mind*—and away they go by the ton. Many people seem to be interested in knowing God for what they can get out of Him.

They do not seem to know that God wants to give Himself. He wants to impart Himself with His gifts. Any gift that He would give us would be incomplete if it were separated from the knowledge of God Himself.

If I should pray for all of the spiritual gifts listed in Paul's epistles and the Spirit of God should see fit to give me all seventeen, it would be extremely dangerous for me if, in the giving, God did not give Himself, as well.

We have mentioned creation and the fact that God has created an environment for all of His creatures. Because God made man in His image and redeemed him by the blood of the Lamb, the heart of God Himself is the true environment for the Christian. If there is grief in heaven, I think it must come from the fact that we want God's gifts, but we don't want God Himself as our environment.

I can only say that if God gives you a rose without giving Himself, He is giving you a thorn. If God gives you a garden without giving Himself, He is giving you a garden with a serpent. If He gives you wine without the knowledge of God Himself,

He is giving you that with which you may destroy yourself.

I feel that we must repudiate this great, modern wave of seeking God for His benefits. The sovereign God wants to be loved for Himself and honored for Himself, but that is only part of what He wants. The other part is that He wants us to know that when we have Him, we have everything—we have all the rest. Jesus made that plain when He said, "Seek ye first the kingdom of God and His righteousness, and all these things shall be added unto you."

It seems that Christian believers have been going through a process of indoctrination and brainwashing, so it has become easy for us to adopt a kind of creed that makes God to be our servant instead of our being God's servant.

Why should a man write and distribute a tract instructing us on "How to Pray So God Will Send You the Money You Need"? Any of us who have experienced a life and ministry of faith can tell how the Lord has met our needs. My wife and I would probably have starved in those early years of ministry if we couldn't have trusted God completely for food and everything else. Of course, we believe that God can send money to His believing children—but it becomes a pretty cheap thing to get excited about the money and fail to give the glory to Him who is the Giver!

So many are busy "using" God. Use God to get a job. Use God to give us safety. Use God to give us peace of mind. Use God to obtain success in business. Use God to provide heaven at last.

Brethren, we ought to learn—and learn it very soon—that it is much better to have God first and have God Himself even if we have only a thin dime than to have all the riches and all the influence in the world and not have God with it!

John Wesley believed that men ought to seek God alone because God is love, and he advised people in his day: "If anyone comes preaching and tells you to seek anything more than love, do not listen, do not listen!" I think in our day we are in need of such an admonition as, "Seek more of God—and seek Him for Himself alone!" If we became serious-minded about this, we would soon discover that all of the gifts of God come along with the knowledge and the presence of God Himself.

Actually, anything or anyone that keeps me from knowing God in this vital and personal way is my enemy. If it is a friend that stands in my way, the friend is an enemy. If it is a gift that stands between us, that gift is an enemy. It may be an ambition, it may be a victory in the past, it may even be a defeat which still overwhelms me—any of these allowed to stand between the Lord and myself becomes an enemy and may keep me from further knowledge of God.

Have you had any part in this cheapening of the Gospel by making God your servant? Have you allowed leanness to come to your soul because you have been expecting that God would come around with a basket giving away presents?

Perhaps some of us have a tendency to think of God standing around and tossing dimes to the children as John D. Rockefeller used to do. Can it be true that Christian believers are engaged in scrambling for those shiny, new dimes and then write a tract about it, such as "I Found a Shiny Dime and It Had the Image of God on It!"

Brethren, let's not try to compare anything like

31

that with the deep and satisfying knowledge of God Himself. Know Him! Go on to know Him! Then, if anyone comes to quote scriptures and argue that your experience is all wrong, you can reply, "You are a good expositor—but I happen to know my Lord, and I love Him just for Himself!"

This is all that the Lord desires for us—and it is in this that we fulfill the purpose for which He created us!

Chapter Three

Always Slamming
on the Brakes!

"The average, modern Christian is not Christ-like. He is quick to defend his flaws, his weaknesses and defeats in fiery, red-faced indignation!"

It seems that we have reached a time in the Christian church when it has become embarrassing to ask plainly and in so many words: "Is there anyone for spiritual perfection?"

It is apparent that many people become nervous and uncomfortable, even in our evangelical Christian circles, when we seek to bring forward this theme of spiritual perfection. I am amazed that Christians can continue to read the strong appeals of the Lord Jesus Christ and the apostles throughout the New Testament for more earnest spiritual desire—and still want to put on the brakes!

What is their concept of Christianity? Do they think it is partly religion and partly play and social fun? Do they reject a true concept of Christianity— that our spiritual life is really a battlefield, a preparation for a greater life to come? If the cross of Jesus Christ means what it should to us and we know that we must carry it and die on it and then rise and live above it, we will have a constant desire to advance and gain spiritual ground!

The nervous people who want to put on the brakes, who feel the necessity for restraint in matters of spiritual desire and yearning for perfection, often use the expression, "Let's not get fanatical about this!"

I can only ask: Is it fanaticism to want to go on until you can perfectly love God and perfectly praise Him?

Is it fanatical to find divine joy leaping up within your heart? Is it fanatical to find the willingness within your being to say, "Yes, Lord! Yes, Lord!" and thus live daily in the will of God so that you are living in heaven while you are living on earth?

If this is fanaticism, then it is the fanaticism of the Old Testament patriarchs and the Law; it is the fanaticism of the psalmist and of the prophets and the New Testament writers as well.

This would have to be the fanaticism that gave us Methodism, that gave us the Salvation Army, the fanaticism that gave birth of Moravianism and the entire Reformation. It is the fanaticism that gave us all the friends of God who held close to the truth, the fanaticism that ultimately brought our own Christian and Missionary Alliance into being.

Throughout the ages, there have been the plain saints, the simple saints, the holy people who would not surrender themselves to the common ways of the world. Unappreciated, often unknown, they were found in many places.

History tells us how they salted down the nations, even in the darkest of times. They set themselves to live by a spiritual perfection, or at least the beginning of spiritual perfection day by day. So it was that when the time of the Reformation came, there was a fertile soil into which to put the seed. Luther, even with his bull neck, could never have done what he did if there had not been a preparation by John Tawler and others like him, going up and down the land preaching this kind of spiritual desire and attainment.

You who study the Word of God know full well that a hunger for God's will is the mood and temper of the Law and of the Psalms and of the prophets and of the New Testament writers.

Those of you who have gone on to read the great books of devotion within the Christian faith know, too, that this yearning for perfection was the temper of all of the superior souls who have ever lived. They have written our great works of faith and love and devotion and they have composed our loftiest hymns. It is to our shame that we as unworthy spiritual descendants of those great fathers so often use their hymns without any spiritual awareness of what we are singing!

This is one of the marks of our modern time— that many are guilty of merely "nibbling" at the truth of the Christian gospel.

I wonder if you realize that in many ways the preaching of the Word of God is being pulled down to the level of the ignorant and spiritually obtuse; that we must tell stories and jokes and entertain and amuse in order to have a few people in the audience? We do these things that we may have some reputation and that there may be money in the treasury to meet the church bills.

I believe in being honest about it—let's admit that we have to pull down the application of the gospel not to the standard of the one who is really thirsting after God, but to the one who is the most carnal, the cheapest saintling hanging on by the teeth anywhere in the kingdom of God!

In many churches Christianity has been watered down until the solution is so weak that if it were poison it would not hurt anyone, and if it were medicine it would not cure anyone!

Now I want to bring you to my postulate that most present-day Christians live sub-Christian lives.

I repeat: Most modern Christians live sub-Christian lives!

Most Christians are not joyful persons because they are not holy persons, and they are not holy persons because they are not filled with the Holy Spirit, and they are not filled with the Holy Spirit because they are not separated persons.

The Spirit cannot fill whom He cannot separate, and whom He cannot fill, He cannot make holy, and whom He cannot make holy, He cannot make happy!

There you have it—my postulate that the modern Christian, even though he has accepted Christ and has been born again, is not a joyful person because he is not a holy person.

My postulate further insists that the average modern Christian is not Christ-like. The proof of this is apparent in the disposition that we find among the children of God. If I did not have some sense of prophetic vision to see down the years, and like the prophets to be willing to fall asleep not having seen the fulfillment of the promises, I would be deeply despondent to know that I have preached for years to some people who still have bad dispositional flaws. In addition, they have moral weaknesses, and suffer frequent defeats. They have a dulled understanding and often live far below the standard of the Scriptures and thus outside the will of God.

The worst of it is that many in this condition will defend their flaws, their weaknesses and defeats in fiery, red-faced indignation!

We should not be too surprised by this substandard spiritual condition, for it is often described in the Bible. You will remember a warning which was spoken concerning Israel, God's people, first in the Old Testament and repeated in the New: though the children of Israel should be as the sand by the seashore in number, only a remnant should be saved.

Our Lord Himself said in the gospel record that the love of many would wax cold. In the letters to the seven churches in the Revelation, we have descriptions of churches that function as churches but have lost their first love and are cold and have very much wrong with them spiritually.

Read in the New Testament and you will find that there were persons who refused completely the teachings of Jesus, even though He lived and served in their midst.

The point I am making here is that there are at least four different and distinct stages of Christian experience and maturity which we consistently find among the professing children of God. Lest there be misunderstanding and misinterpretation, I must make it plain that these are four very evident stages of spiritual life and disposition to be found among us every day—but not four works of grace!

I can just hear someone saying, "I have heard about two works of grace, and I have even heard of some who teach that there are three, but now Tozer is teaching four!"

No, not four works of grace!

I will refer to one of God's great souls of the past and his book, *The Cloud of Unknowing*. We do not know the name of the devoted saint who more than 600 years ago wrote in his pre-Elizabethan English for the purpose, as he declares it, "that God's children might go on to be 'oned' with God."

At the beginning of his book, he breathed a brief prayer of longing and devotion, and I come back to it often for the good of my own spirit.

He said, "Oh God, under whom all hearts be open, and unto whom all will speaketh, and unto whom no privy thing is hid, I beseech Thee, so for to cleanse the intent of my heart with the unspeakable gift of Thy grace, that I may perfectly love Thee and worthily praise Thee!"

In this prayer he first acknowledges that in God's sight all hearts are open and fully known. God can see in, even if you close your heart, or lock it and throw away the key. God still sees into your heart.

"And unto whom all will speaketh"—this is one of the doctrines of the Bible and strongly emphasized in his book, that the will of a man's heart is prayer. Centuries later Montgomery expressed it: "Prayer is the soul's sincere desire unuttered or expressed." In other words, what you will in your heart is eloquent, and God is always listening to what you are willing, what you are determining to do, and what you plan.

"And unto whom no privy thing is hid"—nothing can be held as a secret from the living God.

Then, "I beseech Thee, so for to cleanse the intent of my heart with the unspeakable gift of Thy grace, that I may perfectly love Thee and worthily praise Thee."

I can discern no trace of theological fault or error in this prayer of devotion and desire breathed long ago by this saint of God.

"Oh God, fix my heart so I may perfectly love Thee and worthily praise Thee!" Nothing extreme and fanatical there. The true child of God will say "Amen" to this desire within the being to perfectly love God and worthily praise Him

He points out, "I find four degrees and forms of Christian men's living." He names them: "common," "special," "singular," and "perfect."

He was frank in telling how Christians lived six centuries ago. I think this old saint would have been an outstanding and effective evangelist. If he had come around 600 years later, how we could have used him in our camps and conferences!

He knew the categories among Christians then, and I believe we can see them today.

There are "common" Christians and God knows what a mob we are!

There is also the "special" Christian. He has moved on a little.

Then there is the "singular" Christian, and he is unusual.

But now, this man who is our teacher for the time continues: "These first three stages, common, special and singular, may be begun and ended in this life. But the fourth, the perfect Christian may by the grace of God begin here but shall ever last on without end in the bliss of heaven."

So you see now that neither he nor I are "perfectionists" to the point that we would walk about with a benign St. Francis smile as if to say, "I am perfect; don't bother me!" We will always find that there is ground yet to be taken even though we have entered into the beginning of spiritual perfection.

There is an interesting admonition by the author of *The Cloud of Unknowing* in which he asks that only those who are serious about going on to perfection should read or consider his writings.

He wrote: "Now, I charge thee and I beseech thee, in the name of the Father and of the Son and of the Holy Ghost, that thou neither read this book nor write it nor speak it nor suffer it to be read, except it be such an one as hath by a true will and by a whole intent, purposed him to be a perfect follower of Christ."

He is saying, in other words, "This is such a serious and weighty matter, that no one should fool around with it, or be merely curious or casual about it—only those who have made up their minds and have a true will and a whole intent to be a perfect follower of Jesus Christ."

The old saint then says: "For my intent was never to write such things unto them, therefore, I would that they meddle not herewith, neither they nor any of these curious persons, either lettered or unlettered."

So if the only interest you have in the deeper spiritual life is based on curiosity, it is not enough regardless of your education or scholarship!

In our day we have seen a great revival of interest in mysticism, supposedly a great interest in the deeper life. But I find that much of this interest is academic and based on curiosity. We become interested in aspects of the deeper Christian life much as we become interested in mastering the yo-yo or folk songs or dabbling in Korean architecture or anything else that intrigues us. You can go anywhere now and buy a book about the deeper life because there are curious persons who are swelling the market.

But this saint of old said, "I never want any curious, merely curious person to even bother about this for he will never get anything out of it."

I think I hear him saying to me as well, "Tozer, by the grace of God in the power of the Trinity, I beseech you do not preach this unless people are determined in their hearts to be perfect followers of Christ,"

But it is Jesus' blood that makes the difference and because of this hope that by the blood of Jesus we may be worthy to listen, I differ with the old saint in this point.

Brethren, I am not willing to withhold the open secrets of spiritual power from those who can receive them just because there are others who cannot. I am not going to withhold the open secret of the victorious life from those who can understand it and desire it because of those who are merely curious and without desire. We must leave the sorting out to God. The testing in the matters of spiritual life is by the Spirit of God, not by pastors and preachers.

We have many examples of men and women being tested unconsciously in the scriptures, for the Holy Spirit rarely tells a person that he is about to be tested.

When you go to a doctor for an examination or take a scheduled examination in the classroom, the testing is conscious and purposeful. Consciously and knowingly you are taking a test to find out where you stand or whether you can fulfill the requirements.

But in the scriptures the testing times were very rarely known to those being tested, and that is a sobering thought.

Abraham was being tested when he was asked to leave Ur of the Chaldees, but he did not know it. And when the Lord asked Abraham to take his only son up into the mountain, he thought he was being ordered. He did not know that he was being tested.

Peter was unconsciously tested. Paul was tested. There comes a time when we have heard enough truth and had sufficient opportunity and the Holy Spirit says, "Today this man is going to have his test!"

The people of Israel in their time of testing came to Kadesh-barnea and instead of crossing into the land, they said, "We will not go over." They were unconscious of the testing, and they went back. They did not realize that they were sentencing themselves to forty years of aimless, useless wandering in the desert sands. The Lord had not said to them, "Now stand up, everyone. Breathe deeply! This is going to be a test!" He simply let them make their own test and they flunked it.

It is a solemn and frightening thing in this world of sin and flesh and devils, to realize that about eighty or ninety percent of the people whom God is testing will flunk the test!

The Lord will do His own sorting out, and all of us should be aware that we are in a time when every day is a day of testing. Some come to their Kadesh-barnea and turn back. Some simply stand and look across the river. They are only curious.

Is there anyone for spiritual perfection—anyone with an honest desire to be Christlike—to be more like Jesus Christ every day?

Chapter Four

You Can't Be a Baby All Your Life!

"God is not honored by our arrested development The New Testament teaches that we should go on to full maturity, that mediocrity is not the highest that Jesus offers!"

I have long resisted and argued against the assumption that all Christians are alike and that there are no distinctions that can be made between them.

"All Christians are saints in God's eyes and that is the end of the matter!" I have been told.

I am acquainted with all of the arguments, but they do not satisfy me in the light of the words of Jesus and the teachings of the apostles. I still think that we must preach and instruct and urge men and women who are toiling along in average and common Christian ways to move forward and claim spiritual victory which they have not yet known.

If all Christians are alike in standing and state, why did Jesus Christ talk about three distinctions in the Christian life: "some thirty, some sixty and some a hundred fold"? Why did He say that some will be qualified to rule over many cities and others over few cities? Why did He teach that some should have higher positions than others in the kingdom of God?

If we are all alike and have arrived at the same place and state, why did the Apostle Paul tell the Philippian Christians: "I have suffered the loss of all things, and count them but dung that I may win Christ and be found in him . . . that I may know him, and the power of his resurrection . . . and be conformable unto his death, if by any means I might attain unto that superior resurrection"?

Have you ever pondered the full meaning of the much-quoted verse in the Old Testament, Proverbs 4:18: "The path of the just is as a shining light, that shineth more and more unto the perfect day"?

I have compared this verse in a number of translations. Goodspeed says, "The path of the righteous is like the light of the dawn that shines ever more brightly until the day is full." Rotherham says, "The path of the righteous is like the light of the dawn going on and brightening unto a more radiant day."

This is an inspired utterance concerning a true relationship with God. Through it, the writer is saying to us that when a person becomes a Christian the sun comes up. Then, his experience along the path should be like the appearing of the dawn and the glowing of the light which shineth more and more unto the perfect day.

Christians are very fond of this verse. They memorize it. They quote it—but they don't believe it! If they really believed it they would enter into this experience—"more and more unto the shining of the perfect day!"

I am of the opinion that we cannot experience that which we have not believed. This is the reason why many Christians remain about where they are—day after day, week after week, year after year. Time moves along and special revival speakers come and go. As a result, we have little spells in which we hope to do better. But if we are honest, we must admit that most Christians stay mired down right where they are.

The sad thing is that there are many in our churches who do not have a long time to live. They have grown old and yet they are not one inch farther up the mountain than they were on that day when the sun first arose on them in conversion. In fact, some are not even as far advanced along the way with God as they were a few years ago! It is a sad truth that they have already known a day in the past when their faith was keener, their love warmer, the tears nearer the surface, their love of prayer greater, purity and separation brighter, and the principle within more marked than it is now.

If these things are true, I can only conclude that these are "common" Christians, men and women who do not hear the Lord speaking to them as they should.

God will speak to us if we read and study and obey the Word of God. But when He does speak, we should speak back to Him in prayer and devotion. That which we speak to Him is important, as we can see in the book of Psalms. Here is a man—an inspired man—speaking back to God!

In a similar way, that is why the great devotional

literature is so helpful to us. God has spoken to His saints and they have spoken back to Him, and in His wisdom He has preserved many of these examples for us.

We are taking some suggestions from a 600-year-old volume, *The Cloud of Unknowing*, written by an anonymous saint of God. It was his premise that many among us are common Christians, while others press on into "special" and "singular" and "perfect" stages of Christian life and experience.

"The first three of these may be begun and ended in this life," he wrote. "You can enter into perfection but you cannot enter in fully because the fourth may by grace be begun here but it shall last without end in the bliss of heaven."

I believe that is a perfect response to Paul's expression that "I count not myself to have apprehended, neither were already perfect; but let us therefore as many as be perfect be thus minded." Here is the blessed contradiction—we have entered into perfection, but we have not yet gone all the way!

The Apostle Paul was stretching forth in that light and radiance which shines more and more unto the perfect day. He said that all will be raised from the dead but he pressed forward because of God's promise of a better resurrection out from among the dead.

"Not as though I had already attained, either were already perfect, but I follow after, forgetting the things that are behind," the apostle said.

In the light of Paul's commitment and desire, what shall we say about the shameful mediocrity of the average or common Christian in daily life and experience? What are his reasons for not moving forward in the plan and will of God for his life?

First, consider the definition of the word "common." It means just plain ordinary—of common rank or quality or ability.

A common Christian is one who is of ordinary quality and ability. He is not distinguished by superiority of any kind. He has begun. He does believe. Perhaps he carries a Bible. But he is not distinguished for spiritual attainment.

I must leave it to each of you whether this is a description of your own kind of spirituality as a Christian. Perhaps you are of just common quality, not distinguished in your Christian life in any way. As a result no one will ever want to consult you for guidance or help. No one will ever want to quote you about the things of God.

Mediocre—most Christians are mediocre!

Actually, I hate the word—mediocre! I get no pleasure out of using it, but I think I am telling the truth when I say that it describes many Christians.

The word mediocre comes from two Latin words and literally means "half-way to the peak." This makes it an apt description of the progress of many Christians. They are half-way up to the peak. They are not half-way to heaven but half-way up to where they ought to be, half-way between the valley and the peak. They are morally above the hardened sinner but they are spiritually beneath the shining saint.

Many have settled down right there, and the tragedy is that years ago some of you said, "I am not going to fail God. I am going to push my way up the mountain until I am at the top of the peak, at the highest possible point of experience with God in this mortal life!"

But you have done nothing about it. If anything, you have lost spiritual ground since that day. You are now a half-way Christian! You are lukewarm, neither hot nor cold. You are half-way up to the peak, half-way to where you could have been if you had pressed on.

Do we really think that this half-way Christian life is the best that Christ offers—the best that we can know? In the face of what Christ offers us, how can we settle for so little? Think of all that He offers us by His blood and by His Spirit, by His sacrificial death on the cross, by His resurrection from the dead, by His ascension to the right hand of the Father, by His sending forth of the Holy Ghost!

I know that many are settling for far less than God is waiting to give. They try to stay happy by adding something to their religion that tickles their carnality from the outside. They introduce converted cowboys and half-converted movie actors, and I think they would even stoop to talking horses and gospel dogs to be able to join in saying, "We had a wonderful time!" They will pay a big price to feature some "ninety-day wonder" so they can get the people to crowd in.

Such as these are mediocre Christians. They have not gained the heights where they can feel the warmth of the sun and yet they are not far enough down to be frozen in the valley.

Certainly God is not honored by our arrested development—our permanent half-way spiritual condition. We honor and please Him by going on to full maturity in Christ. We all know that this is what the Bible teaches. Read your New Testament again and you will agree that mediocrity in the Christian life is not the highest that Jesus offers.

Why, then, are we such common Christians? Why have we settled for such shallow pleasures, those little joys that tickle the saintlets and charm the fancy of the carnal?

It is because we once heard a call to take up the cross, and instead of following toward the heights, we bargained with the Lord like a Maxwell Street huckster. We started asking selfish questions and laying down our own conditions.

We had seen the finger of God beckoning. We had been stirred by His Spirit, and all aglow with desire we considered going up to the mountain. We felt an urge to be spent for Christ, to live as near to spiritual perfection as it is possible in this life.

However, instead of going on we started asking questions. We began to bicker and bargain with God about His standards for spiritual attainment.

This is plain truth, not about unbelieving "liberals," but about those who have been born again. We have His life—and yet when He calls us to the heights, we begin to quibble and bargain.

"Lord, what will it cost me?" we ask. "I want to go on but I want to know what it will cost me!"

I am convinced that anyone who brings up the question of consequences in the Christian life is only a mediocre and common Christian. He seems to have completely forgotten that the cross is involved at this point. Jesus himself plainly said, "Take up your cross and follow me and where I am there you will be also. If you will do that the Father will honor you." Jesus said that!

So, the devoted and committed person who takes the cross and follows the Lord does not ask what the consequences will be, neither does he argue about God's plan and God's wisdom.

I have known some who were interested in the deeper life, but hesitated for fear of what such a decision would cost in time, in money, in effort or perhaps in the matter of friendships. These are some of the areas that hinder us.

Now, I do not mean to put down the value and meaning of dear friendships. Human friendships can have a beautiful character that will carry over into the world to come. But the point is that if we ask questions about losing friends when the Lord is dealing with us about spiritual blessing and victory, we are not worthy to be among the saints.

Another question that people ask of the Lord when He calls them to move forward is: "Will it be safe?"

This question comes out of our constant bleating about "security" and our everlasting desire for safety above all else.

We ought to be prepared for the fact that faith has a disturbing element within it. In the days of Luther, when it cost something to be a Christian, the old Lutherans said: "Faith is a perturbing thing."

Dare we face the fact that the Word of God more often than not puts us in a place of peril rather than settling us down easily in a place of security? But most Christians in our day want to dictate to God— they will not accept a place of peril. They do not want to trust.

Some of us have had a delightful experience with a Christian brother from England. He had formerly made money in business and never went anywhere without taking large sums with him. But the Holy Spirit began dealing with him about God's provision and God's resources. Sharing his experience with us, he said: "My wife and I have committed everything to God. We don't even own a house. We have no regular income. I do the work of an evangelist and we are just out doing God's will.

"It is not at all unusual now for us to get in our car and travel several hundred miles with only ten dollars for expenses and not knowing what the next step will be," he told us. "God is spending us. He will not let us down but He is holding us to it so that we will never be able to get our earthly roots in again."

This is the language of the confident Christian who is going on with God. That question, "Is it safe?" is an ignoble question. What is the difference whether it is safe or not as long as He is our Lord?

A third question that we want Him to answer for us is, "Will it be convenient?"

What must our Lord think of us if His work and His witness depend upon the convenience of His people? The truth is that every advance that we make for God and for His cause must be made at our inconvenience. If it does not inconvenience us at all, there is no cross in it! If we have been able to reduce spirituality to a smooth pattern and it costs us nothing —no disturbance, no bother and no element of sacrifice in it—we are not getting anywhere with God. We have stopped and pitched our unworthy tent halfway between the swamp and the peak.

We are mediocre Christians!

Was there ever a cross that was convenient? Was there ever a convenient way to die? I have never heard of any, and judgment is not going to be a matter of convenience, either! Yet we look around for convenience, thinking we can reach the mountain peak conveniently and without trouble or danger to ourselves.

Actually, mountain climbers are always in peril and they are always advancing at their inconvenience.

Still another of those huckster questions that we ask when we hear the voice of Jesus calling us onward is this: "Will it be fun?"

I am sure you know my reaction to this one. No one who asks this question about spiritual advance will ever be anything but a common Christian. He will be mediocre until he dies. He will never be recognized in any way for significant spiritual qualities and he will never be outstanding for any gifts of the Holy Ghost.

It is because there are so many of these ignoble saintlets, these miniature editions of the Christian way, demanding that Christianity must be fun, that distinct organizations have been launched to give it to them. Yes, there are organizations that exist for the sole purpose of mixing religion and fun for our Christian young people.

In answer to this, I happen to know that young people can be just as responsible before God as older people. The youth who meets Jesus and is converted is just as ready and responsible for inconvenience and cost to himself as is the man of seventy. Jesus Christ never offered amusement or entertainment for His disciples, but in our day we have to offer both if we are going to get the people—because they are common Christians.

Because fun and popularity seem to go hand-in-hand, some of the indecisive ask, "Oh Lord, will I still be popular if I follow all the way?"

Ah, the weaklings, the weaklings! They must have the approval and support of the group because they are afraid of standing alone. They want to be able to fit in, seeking a guarantee of solidarity in order to bolster one another in the face of sagging courage. Some just cannot stand alone and when they ask, "Is it popular?", they are avoiding the path of standing alone for God.

I was converted by the grace of God when I was 17 years old and there was no other Christian in my home. It was in the city of Akron and my family took in boarders. We had a house full of people at all times and yet, in the matter of my faith, I was completely alone. I must not leave the impression that I stood as nobly as Stephen in the book of Acts, but I did stand—and it was tough to stand alone. No one else wanted to go to church. No one wanted to pray at the table. No one wanted to read the Bible, but by the good grace of God, I stood alone and I have always been able to thank God for the results.

My mother and father were both converted, as well as two of my sisters. A brother-in-law was converted before he died and several others came to know the Saviour.

What if I had argued: "Lord, is it popular? What will it cost me?" Those persons would never have met the Lord. God stands willing to give us His help by His grace and mercy.

Many who are God's children have probably hesitated at times and tried to bargain with God. They have known Him in conversion. They know that the change came—and yet they bear the marks of mediocrity. But the important thing is this—they are not at the end of God's love!

It is one of the devil's oldest tricks to discourage the saints by causing them to look back at what they were. No one will make progress with God until he lifts up his eyes and stops looking at himself. We are not to spend our time looking back and looking in—we are told to look forward!

Our Lord is more than able to take care of our past. He pardons instantly and forgives completely. His blood makes us worthy—all we are and all we have is by the forgiving love of God!

The goodness of God is infinitely more wonderful than we will ever be able to comprehend. If the root of the matter is in you and you are born again, God is prepared to start with you where you are, and He will not belittle you for your years of common Christianity!

Chapter Five

Stopped Dead
in Your Tracks?

"God says, 'I stand ready to pour a little liquid fire into your being.' We respond, 'No, Lord, that sounds like fanaticism.' Yet we want all the benefits of His cross!"

I blame faulty exposition of the New Testament for stopping many Christians dead in their tracks, causing them to shrug off any suggestion that there is still spiritual advance and progress beckoning them on.

The position of some would-be teachers which insists that when you come into the kingdom of God by faith you immediately have all there is in the kingdom of God is as deadly as cyanide. It kills all hope of spiritual advance and causes many to adopt what I call "the creed of contentment."

Why should a Christian settle down as soon as he has come to know the Lord?

I would have to reply that he must have received faulty counsel and bad exposition of New Testament truth. There is always real joy in the heart of the person who has become a child of God, and proper and sound teaching of the Word of God will awake desire within him to move forward in spiritual adventure with Christ.

But the would-be teacher may tell the new Christian, "You are now complete in Him. The Bible says that and it means that you should just be glad that you are complete and there is nothing more you will ever need!" From that time on any effort to forge ahead for God is put down as some sort of fanaticism. This kind of exposition has brought many Christians into a place of false contentment—satisfied to stay right where they are.

But not so with the Apostle Paul who amazes and humbles us as we read in the third chapter of Philippians of his earnest desire to press forward and to become a special kind of Christian.

With great desire, he wrote: "That I may win Christ"—and yet he already had Christ!

With obvious longing he said, "That I may be found in Him"—and yet he was already in Him. We go to Paul more than to any other writer in the Bible to learn the doctrine of being in Christ and yet Paul humbly and intensely breathed this great desire, "that I may know Him," when he already knew Him!

It was this same Paul who gladly testified, "I am crucified with Christ: nevertheless I live; yet not I, but Christ liveth in me: and the life which I now live in the flesh I live by the faith of the Son of God, who loved me, and gave himself for me."

Yet, because he could never be standing still, he further testified, "I follow after; I press toward the mark. I have not obtained. I am striving to lay hold of that for which Christ laid hold on me!"

How utterly foreign that is to the spirit of modern orthodoxy! How foreign to the bland assurances that because we can quote the text of scripture we must have the experience. This strange textualism that assumes that because we can quote chapter and verse we possess the content and experience is a grave hindrance to spiritual progress. I think it is one of the deadliest, most chilling breezes that ever blew across the church of God!

Too many of us are complete strangers to the desire and the spirit which drove the Apostle Paul forward day by day. "That I may win—that I may know—that I may be found in Him"—these were the words that drove Paul. But now, we are often told that we "have" everything, and that we should just be thankful and "go on to cultivate." I say that the two attitudes are foreign to one another. They do not belong together.

We are told to study the Biblical passages in the Greek. We find out what they mean in English. Then we say, "Well, isn't that fine—isn't that fine!" And that is all we do about it. But Paul said, "I press toward the mark for the prize of the high calling of God in Christ Jesus."

Some have even turned that desire of Paul into a pink cloud. They believe that Paul was talking about a pink cloud which he was going to get when Christ returned. In my opinion, there isn't anything about the return of Christ in that expression of Paul. He was talking about the present, and he was expressing his desire to continue on with Christ. He was talking about experiencing all of that for which Christ had apprehended him.

Why do Christian people in our day purposely turn a deaf ear to the clear appeals in the Word of God concerning spiritual desire and victory?

In some cases it is because they have heard truth which they are not willing to obey. Our Lord is not going to compromise with anyone over the issue of disobedience to truth which He reveals. As a result those who knowingly refuse to obey will be brought to a distinct halt in their spiritual life. If there is something that they will not do for Him, some confession they will not make, something they refuse to straighten out, some act of obedience they will not perform—they will come to a stop and just sit. It is a dead halt—like the breaking of an axle on a truck or car.

People are sitting all around in the church of Christ, just as though the axle had broken, and they have not made any progress for years and years. They are completely stopped by non-obedience.

In other cases, Christians have been side-tracked and rendered useless by their acceptance of a state of chronic discouragement. As a result, they have come to a place of contented rationalization that their condition is normal for all Christians.

These are people who are believers, but they are not believers for themselves. They say they believe in this progressive, victorious Christian life but that it is for others, not for themselves. They have been to every altar, they have been to all of the Bible conferences, but the blessings are for someone else.

Now that attitude on the part of believers is neither modesty nor meekness. It is discouragement resulting from unbelief. It is rather like those who have been sick so long that they no longer believe they can get well. They have lived with the illness so long that it has become a pet and they don't want to lose it because they would no longer have a subject for conversation. They would say that they want to get well, but in fact, they do not.

Jesus is still saying, as He said to the man lying by the gate at the pool, "Wouldst thou be made whole?" Jesus made that man whole and raised him up because he wanted to be healed and delivered. If Jesus had found in him that which He finds in so many Christians today—a chronic state of discouragement—He would have passed him by!

A third reason why many make no progress with God is the fact that they have seen fit to join the cult of respectability. They have learned the art of "becoming adjusted." They have chosen to be cool and proper, poised, self-possessed and well-rounded. They would never want anyone to think that they have taken an extreme position, particularly in religious matters.

We are getting so well-rounded and so broadly symmetrical that we forget that every superior soul that has done exploits for God was considered extreme and in many cases even deranged. We talk about the saintly John Wesley, a learned Oxford man and founder of the Methodists, but we forget that he was such a fiery apostle that they used to throw eggs and rocks at him. His clothes looked fine when he went out but when he came back he needed a tailor. Wesley never put poise and adjustment and respectability above that urgency within his soul to make Christ known with all of His saving and keeping power!

Well, thank God for the Wesleys and all the great souls who have not been afraid of being different!

58

Thank God that there are always a few, and the Bible talks about their being worthy. I know that in Revelation 3:4 it says, "They shall walk with me in white for they are worthy." I am not going to try to persuade you that I know the full meaning, but I know that even in times of backsliding and general coldness of heart there have always been some of God's people who were different. I think there was enough difference in their love and desire and adoration that there would be no question about their walking with Him in white!

Now I wonder if any of you think that I am just trying to whip up spiritual desire in your hearts?

No, I am not trying to whip up desire for the simple reason that I know better. I can agitate you nervously but I cannot put spiritual desire in your being.

The old saint who wrote *The Cloud of Unknowing* expressed it like this: "Our Lord hath of his great mercy called thee and led thee unto him by the desire of thine heart." I have reminded you before that God is always previous, God is always there first, and if you have any desire for God and for the things of God, it is God Himself who put it there.

That old writer continued: "Through the everlasting love of his Godhead, he made thee and wrought thee when thou were not." God was already there—you didn't call up because you were not. And then, "He bought thee with the price of his precious blood when you were lost in Adam." Again, God preceded you—God was previous once more. I believe in prevenient grace, and I don't believe that any person can ever be nudged or pushed or jostled into the kingdom of God or into the deeper life except the Holy Ghost does it. He does it out of the everlasting love of his Godhead, the old saint told us, "so tenderly, he would not suffer thee to be so far from him."

Oh my brothers and sisters! Are we not stirred by the expanse of this great sea of glory in which we Christians find ourselves? "He would not suffer thee to be so far from him." He just wouldn't allow it. He just couldn't stand it. This same God who made us when we were nothing and redeemed us when we were sinners "kindled desire so graciously."

How many of us does that describe? Have any of you ever had a gracious, sudden kindling of desire, when everyone else seemed contented with panel discussions and the usual routine of the church which has to do with externals? How many of us go to church regularly and never feel an extra heartbeat, never any kindling of godly desire? We live like that!

So this kind of desire is not something that can be whipped up—God Himself must put it there. We could never have created ourselves and we could never have redeemed ourselves. We cannot talk ourselves into getting a longing for God. It has to come from God.

When I was a young fellow I spent a little time working as "butcher boy" on the train—riding the old Vicksburg and Pacific and selling peanuts, popcorn, chewing gum and candy, as well as books. I really had to quit because I didn't sell enough—I would often sit and read the books from Vicksburg to the end of the line! But I remember that we did try to stir up some desire for peanuts and popcorn among those passengers. We would go through the coaches and give each person just four or five salted peanuts. No one wanted any when we went through but when we came back, nearly everyone was ready to buy. They had gotten a taste and now they had a desire for peanuts. It was a common trick on the trains.

But we cannot do that for you in spiritual matters.

It is not possible! If you have accepted a common state of spiritual living and you have no deep desire for Him, no man can give it to you. Unless you are willing for God to move in and have His way, you are never going to have spiritual adventures like those who have been explorers in the kingdom of God.

We don't think often enough about all those who have been the prospectors among the hills of God—the spiritual adventurers, the explorers of the kingdom. God wrote in the Bible about them because they were seeking a better land.

Why did Abraham leave Ur of the Chaldees? God promised him spiritual adventures, and he moved out at God's bidding, but it didn't make him a hero at that point.

Think of what the contented people must have said.

"Look at that fool," they said. "What's the matter with him? Everyone else is satisfied to go to the temple once a week and make an offering, but Abraham talks about hearing a voice that said 'get thee into the land which I will show thee.' "

They said, "Abraham, you are a fool!"

But Abraham said, "I heard the Voice, plain and clear, I'm moving out!"

At that point Abraham was no hero. They thought he had lost his mind, that he was at least semi-demented. But you know the rest of the story.

Then there was Moses who could have lived on in the house of his supposed mother in Egypt and perhaps could have become the emperor. But he refused to do it. He got up and left. You know the story and the great list of his spiritual adventures and his favor with God.

Think of the apostles and all of the great souls who have been adventurers. They were not the heroes of the crowd, but they have entered into God's great hall of fame. But something had to happen within each one, an internal fire before it became external. This desire to prospect the hills of God for new lodes of gold had to be inward before it could be outward. These adventurers for God knew the happening on the inside before there was any evidence on the outside.

Far too many people still believe that changes on the outside will take care of the whole matter. How many there are who still think that making outward changes in life and character and habits is all that God expects. Many men have made decisions to enter the ministry or to go to work on some foreign field because of advice and pressures from the outside. That can happen to the outside of a man and never really touch his heart at all.

It can happen. It is entirely in the realm of possibility that a missionary could go to the field and spend a lifetime there and yet never have moved beyond the little patch of ground in his own spiritual life. It is not enough just to go in body, moved by something on the outside. This is a journey for the soul—not just for the feet!

This is why God wants to do something within His people. The great problem of the church today is how we may go on to experience and draw upon that which we have in Christ. But we are not doing much about the problem!

One of my preacher friends wrote me that he had been asked to help in a missionary convention in one of our churches. He was to preach on missions. He said that when he arrived, he found there had been no more spiritual preparation for those meetings than there had been for the first game of the world series. The first night there were about 25 people in attendance but the pastor announced that a good, lively quartet would sing on the following night. My friend wrote that the church was packed. The members of the quartet exchanged jibes, lampooned one another and captured the crowd with their clowning. After singing a song which said, "Let's help God some more," and figuring, I suppose, that they had rescued God from what otherwise would have been a boring evening, they took their guitars and rushed out to another engagement to help God some more.

How will anyone grow in grace around a place like that, I ask you? It makes no difference whether it is one of our churches or some other group, or the largest cathedral in the world, no one could grow in grace in such a situation unless he had a private source. We have the Word of God to which we can go. God has not only called us by His love but has promised a place of pasture for our spiritual good.

But some of God's dear children don't have that longing for His best pastures because in spiritual things they have not found the delight of experiencing within themselves all that Christ has provided.

I used to read from the various religions of the East and I recall a passage in the Hindu writings which said, "You who are busy learning texts and not living them are like the man counting other people's cattle without having a single heifer of his own." I thought that was pretty good for an old Hindu, and I could translate that over into my own version and say, "A lot of professing Christians are busy counting other people's cattle—studying theology and archaeology, anthropology and eschatology —but they don't have one little horny heifer of their own." They have very little from God which is their very own. They only have that which really belongs to someone else. They might write a small tract on what God has done for them, but they could write a huge volume if they would on all that God wants to do for them if they would consent.

God is saying, "I stand ready to pour a little liquid fire into your heart, into your spiritual being!"

We respond: "No, Lord, please excuse me. That sounds like fanaticism—and I would have to give up some things!" So we refuse His desire, even though we want all the benefits of His cross.

There is this thoughtful phrase in *The Cloud of Unknowing:* "He wills thou do but look on Him and let Him alone." Let God alone. In other words, let Him work! Don't stop Him. Don't prevent Him from kindling your heart, from blessing you and leading you out of a common state into that of special longing after Him. You don't have to coax God. He is not like a reluctant father waiting for his child to beg. The blessings are His to give and He waits for us to let Him work.

This is a very hard thing for Americans to do because we are naturally-born "do-it-yourself" artists! We don't just hire a plumber and let him do his work—we stand by and tell him how it should be done. It is amazing really that any American ever lies down and allows the doctor to perform the operation. We always want to get our finger in, and that is the way most Christians behave. We think God does the really hard jobs, but that He is glad to have us along to help out.

"Look on Him—and let Him work, let Him alone." Get your hands down to your side and stop trying to tell God where to cut. Stop trying to make the diagnosis for God. Stop trying to tell God what to give you. He is the Physician! You are the patient.

This is good doctrine, brethren. Dr. A. B. Simpson

shocked and blessed and helped dear people in all Christian groups as he taught this truth down through the years—"let God work! Let Him alone! Take your hands off! It is God that worketh in you!"

Let Him work and your spiritual life will begin to blaze like the rising sun.

Chapter Six

Denominations
Can Backslide, Too!

*"Oh, that we would have a naked intent to know Jesus
Christ! It means putting the world and things and people
beneath our feet, opening our hearts to only one lover—
the Son of God Himself!"*

Our problems of spiritual coldness and apathy
in the churches would quickly disappear if Christian
believers generally would confess their great need
for rediscovering the loveliness of Jesus Christ, their
Saviour.

I have good scriptural ground for constantly em-
phasizing my deep concern that Christians should

again begin to love our Lord Jesus with an intensity of love and desire such as our fathers knew.

What is basically wrong with us when we start to backslide as individuals or as churches and denominations?

Jesus Himself gave us a plain answer when He said, "You have left your first degree of love!" He was not speaking of first love as first in consecutive order, but of the degree of our first love for Him.

These words of Jesus reflect one of our great weaknesses in the Christian churches of our day. The fact that we are not going on to know Christ in rich intimacy of acquaintance and fellowship is apparent—but why are we not even willing to talk about it? We are not hearing anything about spiritual desire and yearning and the loveliness of our Saviour which would break down all barriers if we would move into communion with Him. This appeal is not getting into our books. You don't hear it in radio messages. It is not being preached in our churches.

Can it be that we do not believe that Jesus Christ is capable of a growing and increasing intimacy of fellowship with those who are His own? To become acquainted with God is one thing, but to go on in commitment and to experience God in intensity and richness of acquaintance is something more. The Apostle Paul knew this in his yearning as he said, "I want to know Him in that depth and rich intensity of experience!" Of the many compelling reasons why we ought to know our Saviour better than we do certainly the first is that He is a person, Jesus Christ. We all agree that He is a person, that He is the Eternal Son, but have we gone on to adore Him because He is the source and fountain of everything that you and I are created to enjoy?

He is the fountain of all truth, but He is more—

He is truth itself. He is the source and strength of all beauty, but He is more—He is beauty itself. He is the fountain of all wisdom, but He is more—He is wisdom itself. In Him are all the treasures of wisdom and knowledge hidden away!

Jesus Christ our Saviour is the fountain of all grace. He is the fountain and source of all life, but He is more than that. He could say, "I *AM* the life!" He is the fountain of love, but again, He is far more than that—He is love!

He is resurrection and He is immortality and as one of the adoring song writers said, He is the "brightness of the Father's glory, sunshine of the Father's face."

In another hymn, "Fairest Lord Jesus," there are at least two verses that are not always included, which tell us in candor and realism that when everything else has perished and vanished, we will find it is Jesus alone who abides for aye. One verse says, "Earth's fairest beauty, heaven's brightest splendor, in Jesus Christ unfolded see; all that here shineth quickly declineth before His spotless purity."

There is excitement in true love, and I think that we Christians who love our Saviour ought to be more excited about Who He is and What He is!

A friend of mine has been quite irked because I cannot get excited and steamed up about earthly things. I just cannot stand and strike an attitude of awe when a friend drives up with one of the classy new automobiles. I hear people describing the magnificent new houses that they are building, and they have excitement in their voices. But the Word of God forces me to remember that when you have seen the house or the city that hath foundations and whose builder and maker is God, you cannot really ever get excited again about any house ever built by any man in this world.

It has been said that Abraham could never build a permanent house for himself after he had seen the city whose builder and maker was God. I know I have made up my mind about that city—and I would be willing to live in a tent here because I have some idea about my future home up there. I am convinced that it will be beautiful and satisfying beyond anything I can know down here. It is a tragedy if we forget that "earth's fairest beauty and heaven's brightest splendor are all unfolded in Jesus Christ, and all that here shineth quickly declineth before His spotless purity."

The man who wrote those words, breathed them from his soul, must have been one of God's special kind of Christians. He must have known Jesus Christ intimately day by day. He probably knew all about the cost of knowing the Saviour in this way.

But people are not willing to pay that price, and that is why so many Christians must be described as "common." Most Christians talk piously about the cost of Christianity in terms of the unclean, injurious and grossly sinful things they have "surrendered." But if they never get beyond that they are still common Christians. They talk about having given up the bad things, but the Apostle Paul said that for Christ's sake he surrendered the good things as well as the bad.

"What things were gain to me I count but loss," he said. He meant things to which he still had a legal and moral right, things about which he could have said, "These are mine and Christianity is not going to take them from me!"

"I yield them all, I give them all because I have found That which is so much better," he wrote. He had found "That" which was with the Father, Jesus Christ, the fountain from Whom flows all wisdom and beauty and truth and immortality!

Paul knew something that many Christians still have not learned—that the human heart is idolatrous and will worship anything it can possess. Therein lies the danger of the "good" things. We have surrendered evil things, bad things, but we hold on to the good things and these we are prone to worship. Whatever we refuse to surrender and count but loss we will ultimately worship. It may be something good, but it gets between you and God—whether it be property or family or reputation or security or your life itself.

Jesus warned us about our selfishness in grasping and hanging on to our own lives. He taught that if we make our life on earth so important and so all-possessing that we cannot surrender it gladly to Him, we will lose it at last. He taught that plainly, and He also warned us about trusting earthly security rather than putting our complete confidence in God.

We all want a guarantee of security, but we didn't get that idea from the Apostle Paul. He was hardly ever secure as far as the things of this life were concerned. He said he died daily. He was always in difficulty, whether with the governments of this world or with the stormy elements on the sea.

Brethren, we want security in this life and eternal security in the world above! I think that is a kind of definition of our modern-day Christian fundamentalism. But Paul said, "I have been captured by Jesus Christ so I disavow and disown everything."

Now there were certain things that God let Paul have. He let him have a book or two. He let him have a garment, a cloak. In one instance, He let him have his own hired house for two years. But the example Paul gave us was the fact that any "things" which God allowed him to have never touched him at heart, at the point of possession.

Any of our external treasures which really bind us at heart will become a curse. Paul said, "I give them up that I might know Him." He never allowed things to become important enough to mar his relationship with God.

The example and admonitions of Paul cause me to call into question some of the teachings in our current Christian circles that Christ is something "added on"—that by ourselves we can have a rather jolly earthly life, but we also need Jesus to save us from hell and to get us into the mansions on the other side!

Now, that is not New Testament teaching and certainly not the way in which Paul looked at things in this world. Paul said that he found Jesus Christ so infinitely attractive that he was forced to throw out every set of values established on earth.

Paul was a learned man, an intellectual educated at the feet of Gamaliel. We would have honored him as a Ph.D. But Paul said, "That is all dross." His expression actually meant: "It is a kind of garbage."

Paul spoke of his birth and of his register and standing among the fathers of his religious heritage and then testified that "for the sake of Jesus Christ, I count it nothing at all—I put it under my feet."

That ought to say something to us who have so many things about which we are proud. Some of us boast about our national and cultural forebears until we actually become carnal about it. We are proud of things and proud of what we can do. But Paul said, "Everything about which I could be proud as a man I count but loss for the sake of Jesus Christ."

So Paul gives us the proper motives for loving and following the Saviour and for giving up the things that would hold us back. Modern Christianity has a lot to learn from Paul in this area of motives.

Because of the nature of our times, some are insisting: "America, you had better turn to God or that final bomb will get you!" Another voice of alarm warns: "America, you had better stop drinking and gambling or you will go down like Rome!"

Our old teacher-friend, *The Cloud of Unknowing,* gives us some light on proper motives in relationship to the nature of God Himself. "God is a jealous lover and He suffereth no rival," this saint wrote more than 600 years ago. "God cannot work in our wills unless He can possess our wills for Himself."

Now brethren, this is one of our greatest faults in our Christian lives. We are allowing too many rivals of God. We actually have too many gods. We have too many irons in the fire. We have too much theology that we don't understand. We have too much churchly institutionalism. We have too much religion. Actually, I guess we just have too much of too much!

God is not in our beings by Himself! He cannot do His will in us and through us because we refuse to put away the rivals. When Jesus Christ has cleansed everything from the temple and dwells there alone, He will work!

God wants to do His work hidden and unseen within the human breast. Have you ever been deep down in a mine in the earth? They are mining out coal or gold or diamonds, but anyone flying or walking or traveling overhead may have no idea of what is going on in the depths of that hill. They would never know that deep within the earth there is an intelligent force at work bringing out jewels. That is what God does deep within us—and He works hidden and unseen.

But in our day we must be dramatic about everything. We don't want God to work unless He can make a theatrical production of it. We want Him

72

to come dressed in costumes with a beard and with a staff. We want Him to play a part according to our ideas. Some of us even demand that He provide a colorful setting and fireworks as well!

That is how we want it, but God says, "No, no, no! You children of Adam, you children of carnality and lust, you who love a fair showing of flesh, you who have wrong ideas about my Son, I cannot do my work according to your prescription. I cannot do my work in you!"

How can God do His work in people who seem to think that Christianity is just another way of getting things from God?

I hear people testify that they give their tithe because God makes their nine-tenths go farther than the ten-tenths. That is not spirituality; that is just plain business. I insist that it is a dangerous thing to associate the working of God with our prosperity and success down here. I cannot promise that if you will follow the Lord you will soon experience financial prosperity, because that is not what He promised His disciples. Down through the years, following the Lord has meant that we count all things but loss for the excellency of the knowledge of Christ.

"And don't some Christians prosper?" you ask.

We have many examples of Christian men whom God has been able to trust with unusual prosperity and as they continue to follow the Lord, they give most of it back to Him. But they haven't made Christianity just a technique of getting things.

I hear people testify about their search for the deeper Christian life and it sounds as though they would like to be able to get it in pill form. It seems that it would have been much more convenient for them if God had arranged religion so they could take it like a pill with a glass of water. They buy books, hoping to get their religion by prescription. But there isn't any such thing. There is a cross. There is a gallows. There is a man with bleeding stripes on his back. There is an apostle with no property, with a tradition of loneliness and weariness and rejection and glory—but there are no pills!

There are a thousand ways in which we try to use the Lord. What about that young fellow studying for the ministry, studying until his eyesight begins to fail, but he wants to use Jesus Christ to make him a famous preacher. They will ordain him, and he will get the title of Reverend and if he writes a book, they will make him a Doctor. But if he has been using Jesus Christ, he is just a common huckster buying and selling and getting gain, and the Lord would drive him out of the temple along with the rest.

Then there are some among us these days who have to depend upon truckloads of gadgets to get their religion going, and I am tempted to ask: What will they do when they don't have the help of the trappings and gadgets? The truck can't come along where they are going!

I heard a man boasting on his radio program about the equipment they were going to bring in from Pennsylvania and Ohio so they could better serve the Lord. I don't know of any fancy kind of equipment which will brighten your testimony or your service for God.

I think of the dear old camp meeting ladies who used to say, "This is my harp of ten strings, and I praise the Lord!" I can see in my mind now those wrinkled hands with brown spots, but as they clapped those wrinkled, aging hands how their faces would shine! And their harp? Just those hands as they clapped and sang praises to God.

Who needs a bushel basket full of clap-trap in order to serve the Lord? You can worship God anywhere if you will let Him work in your being and suffer no rival. You may be still with arthritis so that you can't even get on your knees to pray, but you can look up in your heart, for prayer isn't a matter of getting on your knees. Prayer is the elevation of the heart to God and that is all a man needs to praise, to pray and to worship.

Now here is a strange thing. If you talk about mysticism in our day, every fundamentalist throws his hands high in the air with disgust to let you know that he considers the mystics dreamers, those who believe in the emotion and feeling. But all of those old saints and the fathers of whom I have read taught that you must believe God by a naked, cold intent of your will and then the other things follow along. ―

A naked intent unto God—those old saints were practical men. They have exhorted us to press on in faith whether we feel like it or not. They have exhorted us to pray—when we feel like it and when we don't. They never taught that we would always be lifted emotionally to the heights. They knew that there are times when your spiritual progress must be by a naked intent unto God.

Oh that we would have this naked intent to know God, to know Jesus Christ! To be able to put the world and things and people beneath our feet and to open our hearts to only one lover, and that the Son of God Himself!

Oh for the proper balance in all of our relationships! Husband and wife, father and son, mother and daughter, business man and partner, taxpayer and citizen—all of these in their proper place; but in the deep of the heart having only the One lover, He who suffers no rival.

75

Why has God insisted that it should be this way?

Because it is His intention that our understanding and our reason should be broken down and that our whole case should be thrown back on God. Many have known the time of darkness and oppression as they sought to go on with God and to be filled with His fullness. You believed God and you trusted Christ. Whether you felt like it or not, you went on and you believed and you obeyed. You prayed whether you felt like it or not. You straightened things out and you got adjusted in your relationships at home and in business. You quit the wrong things, the things that had been hindering you, whether you felt like it or not. This is faith—a naked intent unto God, and I must tell you this: out of our darkness and out of our stony grief, God will raise a Bethel. Out of the tomb, He will lift you into the sky. Out of darkness, He will lift you into the light!

This is what it means to love Jesus, to know Him just for Himself. How I pray that we may again recapture in our day the glory that men may have known of the beauty of Jesus.

In *The Cloud of Unknowing*, the old saint wrote that because God is a jealous lover, He wants us to be unwilling to think on anything but God Himself.

Now, this was the message of Dr. A. B. Simpson. He shocked and blessed a generation because of his central message: "Jesus—Himself!"

Dr. Simpson was asked to go to England to preach in a Bible conference. He discovered that he was to preach the third of three messages on sanctification—and that is a bad spot to be in. The first fellow said in his sermon that the way to be holy and victorious in the Christian life is to suppress "the old man." His was the position of sanctification by suppression. The second man got up and took the position of eradication, deliverance from the old carnal life by eradication. "Get rid of the old man, pull him up, turn up the roots in the sun to die!"

Doctor Simpson had to get in between there and he took just one word for his text: "Himself." Then he gave his testimony of efforts and struggles to get the victory. He said, "Sometimes I would think I had gotten it, and then I would lose it. What a blessedness when I came to the knowledge that I had been looking in the wrong place, when I found that victory, sanctification, deliverance, purity, holiness- all must be found in Jesus Christ Himself, not in some formula. When I claimed Jesus just for Himself, it became easy and the glory came to my life."

Out of that knowledge and out of that blessing, Dr. Simpson wrote his famous hymn, "Once it was the blessing, now it is the Lord. Once His gift I wanted, now Himself alone."

This is the basic teaching of the deeper Christian life. It is the willingness to let Jesus Christ Himself be glorified in us and through us. It is the willingness to quit trying to use the Lord for our ends and to let Him work in us for His glory.

That is the kind of revival I am interested in and the only kind—the kind of spiritual reviving and renewing that will cause people to tremble with rapture in the presence of the Lord Jesus Christ.

"Once it was the blessing—now it is the Lord!"

Chapter Seven

Dark, Dark Night
of the Soul!

"Remember how they nailed Jesus to a cross. Remember the darkness, the hiding of the Father's face. This was the path Jesus took to immortal triumph. As He is, so are we in this world!"

I am convinced that in New Testament Christianity the object of the Holy Spirit is twofold. First, He wants to convince Christians that it is actually possible for us to know the beauty and perfection of Jesus Christ in our daily lives. Second, it is His desire to lead us forward into victory and blessing even as Joshua once led Israel into the promised land.

The first is not too difficult. Most Christians will honestly confess that there are still spiritual frontiers before them which they have not been willing to explore. There is still ground to be taken if our object is to know Christ, to win Christ, to know the power of His resurrection, to be conformed to His death. If our object is to experience within our beings all of those things that we have in Christ judicially, we must come to the place of counting all things loss for the excellency of this knowledge.

We know our lack, but we are very slow in allowing the Holy Spirit to lead us into deeper Christian life and experience, that place where the intent of our heart is so cleansed that we may perfectly love God and worthily praise Him. In spite of our hesitation and delay and holding back God does not give up, because the Holy Spirit is faithful and kind and patient and ever seeks to lead us forward into the life of the special kind of Christian.

I well remember the caution of one of the old saints I have read who pointed out that "a persuaded mind and even a well-intentioned heart may be far from exact and faithful practice" and "nothing has been more common than to meet souls who are perfect and saintly in speculation."

Jesus did not say, "You will be my disciples by speculation." He did say that by your fruit and by your behaviour you will be known. This is one rule that is never deceiving, and it is by this that we should judge ourselves.

God will sift out those who only speculate about the claims of Christ and He will lead forward those who by His grace see Him in His beauty and seek Him in His love.

The story of Gideon is an illustration of how God seeks His qualities within us and is not concerned with us just as numbers or statistics. Gideon was about to face the enemy and he had an army of 32,000 soldiers. But the Lord said to Gideon, "You have too many—let all who are afraid go back." So Gideon gave the word to the troops, and 22,000 of those men turned back. Then the Lord said to Gideon again, "There are still too many. I can see those among you who are not prepared for what we are going to do. You will never be able to make Israelite soldiers of them."

I presume that there are few preachers among us on the top side of this terrestrial ball who would have turned down those 22,000, but God was putting the emphasis on quality, on those who would cooperate in the performance of the will of God.

Then Gideon took the 10,000 men to the river and tested them as God had directed and when this sifting was all done, Gideon had an army of 300 men. God seeks out those who are willing that their lives should be fashioned according to His own grace and love. He sifts out those who cannot see God's purpose and design for our blessing.

Some of you know something of that which has been called "the dark night of the soul." Some of you have spiritual desire and deep longing for victory but it seems to you that your efforts to go on with God have only brought you more bumps and more testings and more discouragement. You are tempted to ask, "How long can this go on?"

Let me remind you of the journey of Jesus Christ to immortal triumph. Remember the garden where He sweat blood. Remember Pilate's hall where they put on Him the purple robe and smote Him. Remember His experience with His closest disciples as they all forsook Him and fled. Remember the journey up the hill to Calvary. Remember how they nailed

Him to a cross, those six awful hours, the hiding of the Father's face. Remember the darkness and remember the surrender of His spirit in death. This was the path that Jesus took to immortal triumph and everlasting glory, and as He is, so are we in this world!

Yes, there is a dark night of the soul. There are few Christians willing to go into this dark night and that is why there are so few who enter into the light. It is impossible for them ever to know the morning because they will not endure the night.

In *The Cloud of Unknowing*, we have been told: "This work asketh no long time before it be truly done, as some men think, for it is the shortest work of all that men may imagine. It is neither longer nor shorter, but even according to the stirring that is within thee, even thy will."

The stirring within us often is not enough. There are too many other factors—there is not yet a vacuum within, a prepared place into which the Holy Spirit may come and be at home.

I think the more we learn of God and His ways and of man and his nature we are bound to reach the conclusion that we are all just about as holy as we want to be. We are all just about as full of the Spirit as we want to be. Thus when we tell ourselves that we want to be more holy but we are really as holy as we care to be, it is small wonder that the dark night of the soul takes so long!

The reason why many are still troubled, still seeking, still making little forward progress is because they have not yet come to the end of themselves. We are still giving some of the orders, and we are still interfering with God's working within us.

We struggle to keep up a good front, forgetting that God says the most important thing is for us to

81

be humble and meek as Christ gave us example. It seems that Christians are obsessed with keeping up that good front. We say we want to go to heaven when we die to see old Jordan roll, but we spend most of our time and energy down here just putting on that good front. It seems that many of us say to God, as did King Saul the apostate before us, "Oh God, honor me now before these people!"

We also are guilty of hiding our inner state. The Bible plainly tells us to expose our inner state to God, but we would rather cover it up. God cannot change it if we cover it and hide it.

We disguise the poverty of our spirit. If we should suddenly be revealed to those around us on the outside as Almighty God sees us within our souls, we would become the most embarrassed people in the world. If that should happen, we would be revealed as people barely able to stand, people in rags, some too dirty to be decent, some with great open sores. Some would be revealed in such condition that they would be turned out of Skid Row. Do we think that we are actually keeping our spiritual poverty a secret, that God doesn't know us better than we know ourselves? But we will not tell Him, and we disguise our poverty of spirit and hide our inward state in order to preserve our reputation.

We also want to keep some authority for ourselves. We cannot agree that the last, the final key to our lives should be turned over to Jesus Christ. Brethren, we want to have dual controls—let the Lord run it but keep a hand on the controls just in case the Lord should fail!

We are willing to join heartily in singing, "To God Be the Glory," but we are strangely ingenius in figuring out ways and means by which we keep some of the glory for ourselves. In this matter of perpetually seeking our own interests, we can only say that people who want to live for God often arrange to do very subtly what the worldly souls do crudely and openly.

A man who doesn't have enough imagination to invent anything will still figure out a way of seeking his own interests, and the amazing thing is that he will do it with the help of some pretext which will serve as a screen to keep him from seeing the ugliness of his own behaviour.

Yes, we have it among professing Christians—this strange ingenuity to seek our own interest under the guise of seeking the interests of God. I am not afraid to say what I fear—that there are thousands of people who are using the deeper life and Bible prophecy, foreign missions and physical healing for no other purpose than to promote their own private interests secretly. They continue to let their apparent interest in these things to serve as a screen so that they don't have to take a look at how ugly they are on the inside.

So we talk a lot about the deeper life and spiritual victory and becoming dead to ourselves—but we stay very busy rescuing ourselves from the cross. That part of ourselves that we rescue from the cross may be a very little part of us, but it is likely to be the seat of our spiritual troubles and our defeats.

No one wants to die on a cross—until he comes to the place where he is desperate for the highest will of God in serving Jesus Christ. The Apostle Paul said, "I want to die on that cross and I want to know what it is to die there, because if I die with Him I will also know Him in a better resurrection." Paul was not just saying, "He will raise me from the dead"—for everyone will be raised from the dead. He said, "I want a superior resurrection, a resurrection like Christ's." Paul was willing to be crucified with Christ, but in our day we want to die a piece at a time, so we can rescue little parts of ourselves from the cross.

There are men and women who beg and plead for God to fill them with Himself for they know it would be for their good, but then they stubbornly resist like our own spoiled children when they are not well and they want us to help them.

You try to take the child's temperature or give him medicine or call for a doctor and he will resist and howl and bawl. In the next breath he will beg for help, "Mama, I'm sick!" But he won't take a thing, he won't let you help. He is stubborn and spoiled.

People will pray and ask God to be filled—but all the while there is that strange ingenuity, that contradiction within which prevents our wills from stirring to the point of letting God have His way.

It is for this reason that I do not like to ask congregations to sing one of the old songs, "Fill Me Now." I think it is one of the most hopeless songs ever written—gloomy and hopeless. I have yet to find anyone who was ever filled while singing "Fill me now, fill me now, fill me now." It just doesn't work that way—for if you are resisting God, you can sing all four verses and repeat the last one in a mournful melody but God will still have to wait for your decision on that part of yourself that you are saving from the cross.

Those who live in this state of perpetual contradiction cannot be happy Christians. A man who is always on the cross, just piece after piece, cannot be happy in that process. But when that man takes his place on the cross with Jesus Christ once and for all, and commends his spirit to God, lets go of everything and ceases to defend himself—sure, he has died, but there is a resurrection that follows!

If we are willing to go this route of victory with Jesus Christ, we cannot continue to be mediocre Christians, stopped half-way to the peak. Until we give up our own interests, there will never be enough stirring within our beings to find His highest will.

Why, then, does it take so long? Whose fault is it that we do not have the intents of our heart so cleansed that we may perpetually love Him and worthily serve Him, and that we may be filled with His Spirit and walk in victory?

I hope I have made it plain that it is our fault —and not God's! "This work asketh no long time before it be truly done, as some men think, for it is the shortest work of all that men may imagine, according to the stirring that is within thee, even thy will." If you are one of the fellows who is convinced it has to take a long time, you are wrong. It may be one of the quickest, shortest works that a man may know—just as short or as long as your own will decrees.

Many of us are hanging on to something, something that we hold dear to ourselves, something that comes between us and the Lord.

Some of you as young people may have a tiny baby that has now become your dearest treasure on earth. Perhaps you have heard the still small voice of the Lord saying, "Will you commit that tiny life back to me? Will you take your own hands from the direction of that life and put that direction over into the hands of the Holy Spirit?"

God deals with us all about His highest will for ourselves and for our children. Years ago when our two oldest boys were small I was away from home on a preaching mission. God dealt with me plainly about my possessiveness of the treasure which I had in those two sons. God spoke to me and asked me if I would give them up to Him, and I thought He meant that He wanted them to die. I was prostrate on the floor beside my bed and kicked my toes on the carpet and cried out to God—and I finally gave those two boys back to God. I have been able to see since then in raising those boys and the rest of the children that God doesn't ask for our children for Himself—He just wants to bring us out into a place of surrender so that our children and our earthly possessions do not possess our wills to the point of worship. God puts us through these times because there ought not to be anything in our earthly lives that we would knowingly hold back from God.

I confess that I went through this matter of dying after each child that God gave us. When our little girl came to us, we dedicated her to the Lord in a morning service, but that was nothing. My own personal dedication of that child was a prolonged, terrible, sweaty thing. I finally said to God, "Yes, Lord, you can have her." I knew that God wasn't going to let her die, for I had learned that lesson years before with her two older brothers.

But the thing was this—I didn't know what He wanted, and it was a struggle to give up, to yield.

Later, in giving a testimony in our church, I said, "The dearest thing we have in the world is our little girl, but God knows that He can have her whenever He wants her."

After the service someone came and said, "Mr. Tozer, aren't you afraid to talk like that about your little girl?"

"Afraid?" I said. "Why, I have put her in the hands of perfect love and love cannot wound anyone and love cannot hurt anyone. I am perfectly content that she is shielded in the life of Jesus Christ, His name being love and His hands being strong and His face shining like the beauty of the sun and His heart being the tender heart of God in compassion and lovingkindness."

We who are Christians go through these times of testing and proving as our Lord seeks to deal with us about our treasures possessing us on this earth. With some it may be the commitment of a favorite boy friend or girl friend to God for His highest will. Some people have put life's highest value upon their job and their security in this life. With some it may be a secret ambition, and it is driving a wedge between you and the Lord. Others may be possessed by the amount of your nice little nest egg lying there in the bank, and you just cannot bring yourself to quit calling it yours. You just cannot let go and that is in spite of the fact that you know you can perfectly trust the Lord and the leading of His Spirit.

Do you remember a rather comic character by the name of Sancho Panza in that well-known book, *Don Quixote?* There is an incident in the book in which Senor Panza clung to a window sill all night, afraid that if he let go he would plunge and die on the ground below. But when the morning light came, red-faced and near exhaustion, he found that his feet were only two inches above the grass. Fear kept him from letting go, but he could have been safe on the ground throughout the long night.

I use that illustration to remind us that there are many professing Christians whose knuckles are white from blindly hanging on to their own window sill. The Lord has been saying, "Look on me and let go!" But they have refused.

Paul said we should be "reaching forth unto those things which are before"—but many are afraid.

Happy are the men and women who have given God His way—they "press toward the mark of the prize of the high calling of God in Christ Jesus."

Chapter Eight

God Heard Elijah
Because Elijah Heard God!

"Oneness with Christ means to be identified with Him in crucifixion—then going on to be identified with Him in resurrection power!"

We urgently need a new kind of reformation throughout our Christian churches—a reformation that will cause us not only to accept the will of God but to actively seek it and adore it!

At one point in history concerned believers sought a reformation that would bring the Bible back to the church. They got it.

Again, the church needed a reformation that

would demonstrate that men could be forgiven, converted and transformed. This came about in reality under the Wesleys.

The reformation we need now can best be described in terms of spiritual perfection—which reduced to its simplest form is no more and no less than doing the will of God! This would expose us all at the point of our need, no matter how sound we think we are in doctrine and no matter how great our reputations.

I long for the positive and genuine renewal which would come if the will of God could be totally accomplished in our lives. Everything that is unspiritual would flee, and all that is not Christlike would vanish, and all that is not according to the New Testament would be rejected.

If this ever happens, it will come because Christians are finally willing to look on the Saviour and let Him work, and each will take his own cross with such gladness that he can breathe, "Oh cross, oh good cross, I embrace thee!"

As believers, our relation to the will of God may be twofold: passive and active. In the passive sense we are resigned to God's acts, and in our day when we mention the will of God, we almost invariably mean this kind of resignation to God's will.

We see this resignation in the New Testament account in which God revealed Himself to Mary. He told her what He was going to do and Mary said, "Be it unto me even as Thou wilt." God promised that He would perform a great miracle and she accepted it as the will of God, indeed.

But the second aspect of the will of God is one which we rarely consider—the active side of the will of God. Do we voluntarily and actively observe God's commandments, making positive changes in our lives as God may indicate in order to bring the entire life into accord with the New Testament?

That is the active aspect of the will of God that I would own as reformation in the church, and it would surely result in revival.

Many are content to sit around in the pews singing, "Have Thine Own Way, Lord." They are resigned to this interpretation of the will of God: "Whatever God wants to do is fine with me." They are passively resigned.

But are they willing to hear the voice of God and obey His bidding and do what He wants them to do? That would become active participation and acceptance of the will of God. It would mean bringing the entire life into accord with New Testament teaching.

Some people in reading the Bible say they cannot understand why Elijah and other men had such active power with the living God. It is quite simple. God heard Elijah because Elijah had heard God. God did according to the word of Elijah because Elijah had done according to the word of God. You cannot separate the two.

When we are willing to consider the active will of God for our lives, we come immediately to a personal knowledge of the cross, because the will of God is the place of blessed, painful, fruitful trouble!

The Apostle Paul knew about that. He called it "the fellowship of Christ's sufferings." It is my conviction that one of the reasons we exhibit very little spiritual power is because we are unwilling to accept and experience the fellowship of the Saviour's sufferings, which means acceptance of His cross.

How can we have and know the blessed intimacy of the Lord Jesus if we are unwilling to take the route which He has demonstrated? We do not have it because we refuse to relate the will of God to the cross.

All of the great saints have been acquainted with the cross—even those who lived before the time of Christ. They were acquainted with the cross in essence because their obedience brought it to them.

All Christians living in full obedience will experience the cross and find themselves exercised in spirit very frequently. If they know their own hearts, they will be prepared to wrestle with the cross when it comes.

Think of Jacob in the Old Testament and notice the direction from which his cross came—directly from his own carnal self. It took Jacob some time to discover the nature of his own heart and to admit and confess that Jacob's cross was Jacob himself.

Read again about Daniel and you will discover that his cross was the world. Consider Job and you will find that his cross was the devil. The devil crucified Job, the world crucified Daniel, and Jacob was crucified on the tree of his own Jacobness, his own carnality.

Study the lives of the apostles in the New Testament and you will find that their crosses came from the religious authorities.

Likewise in church history we look at Luther and note that his cross came from the Roman church which makes so much of wooden crosses, while Wesley's cross came from the Protestant church. Continue to name the great souls who followed the will of God, and you will name the men and women of God who looked forward by faith and their obedience invariably led them into places of blessed and painful and fruitful trouble.

I must point out here the fallacy of thinking that in following Jesus we can easily go up on the hillside and die—just like that! I admit that when Jesus was here on earth, the easiest and cheapest way to get off was to follow Jesus physically. Anyone could get out of work and say goodbye with the explanation, "I am going to follow Jesus." Multitudes did this. They followed Him physically, but they had no understanding of Him spiritually. Therefore, in that day the cheapest, easiest way to dispose of the cross was to carry it physically.

But, brethren, taking our cross is not going to mean the physical act of following Jesus along a dusty pathway. We are not going to climb the hill where there are already two crosses in place and be nailed up between them.

Our cross will be determined by whatever pain and suffering and trouble which will yet come to us because of our obedience to the will of God. The true saints of God have always borne witness that wholehearted obedience brings the cross into the light quicker than anything else.

Oneness with Christ means to be identified with Christ, identified with Him in crucifixion. But we must go on to be identified with Him in resurrection as well, for beyond the cross is resurrection and the manifestation of His Presence.

I would not want to make the mistake of some preachers who have never gotten beyond the message of death, death, death! They preach it so much that they never get anyone beyond death into resurrection life and victory.

I recall that when I was a young man and getting along well spiritually, having been wonderfully filled with the Holy Spirit, I read a book about the cross. In that volume, the author put you on the cross in the first chapter, and you were still hanging on the cross in the last chapter. It was gloomy all the way through—and I had a difficult time shaking that off because it was death, death, death! I was greatly helped at that time by the radiant approach of Dr. A. B. Simpson to the meaning of the cross and death to self. He took one through the meaning of the cross to the understanding that beyond the cross there is resurrection life and power, an identification with a risen Saviour and the manifestation of His loving Presence.

The old fifteenth century saint whom we have quoted declared that "God is ingenius in making us crosses."

Considering that, we have to confess that when Christians say, "I am crucified with Christ by faith," they are merely using a technical term and are not talking about a cross in reality. But God wants His children to know the cross. He knows that only spiritual good can come to us as a result of our identification with the Lord Jesus. So, He is ingenius in making crosses for us.

The quotation continues: "He may make them of iron and of lead which are heavy of themselves. He makes some of straw which seem to weigh nothing, but one discovers that they are no less difficult to carry. A cross that appears to be of straw so that others think it amounts to nothing may be crucifying you through and through.

"He makes some with gold and precious stones which dazzle the spectators and excite the envy of the public but which crucify no less than the crosses which are more despised."

Christians who are put in high places, Christians who are entrusted with wealth and influence, know something about the kind of cross that may seem dazzling to spectators and excites the envy of the public—but if they know how to take it, it crucifies them no less than the others.

It seems that He makes our crosses of all the things we like the best so that when they turn to bitterness we are able to learn the true measure of eternal values.

It appears, also, that it often pleases God to join physical weakness to this servitude of the Spirit.

"Nothing is more useful than these two crosses together," the quote from the old saint continues. "They crucify a man from head to foot."

I confess that when I read that it came like a shock to my soul, realizing anew that Jesus Christ was crucified from head to foot! When they nailed Him there, He was crucified in every part of His body and there was no part of His holy nature that did not suffer the full intensity of those pains on the cross.

The children of God must be ready for everything the cross brings or we will surely fail the test! It is God's desire to so deal with us about all of the things that the world admires and praises that we will see them in their true light. He will treat us without pity because He desires to raise us without measure—just as He did with His own Son on the cross!

The Apostle Paul gave us this wonderful assessment of the will of God concerning the person and the earthly work of Jesus Christ: "Let this mind be in you, which was also in Christ Jesus: who, being in the form of God, thought it not robbery to be equal with God: but made himself of no reputation, and took upon him the form of a servant, and was made in the likeness of men: and being found in fashion as a man, he humbled himself, and became obedient unto death, even the death of the cross."

But notice the next word: "Wherefore."

"Wherefore God also hath highly exalted him, and given him a name which is above every name: that at the name of Jesus every knee should bow . . . and every tongue should confess!"

This is why I believe that God will crucify without pity those whom He desires to raise without measure! This is why we believers have to surrender to Him the full control of everything that we consider to be an asset in terms of human power and talent and accomplishment. God takes pleasure in confounding everything that comes under the guise of human power—which is really weakness disguised! Our intellectual power, our great mind, our array of talents—all of these are good if God has so ordered, but in reality they are human weaknesses disguised. God wants to crucify us from head to foot—making our own powers ridiculous and useless—in the desire to raise us without measure for His glory and for our eternal good.

Dare we realize what a gracious thing it is that the Lord of all creation is desirous of raising us into a position of such glory and usefulness? Can we conceive that God would speak to angels and all the creatures who do His will and say of us: "The lid is off for this child of mine! There is to be no ceiling, no measure on what he can have, and there is no limit to where I may take him. Just keep it open. Without measure I will raise him because without pity I have been able to crucify him!"

You who are parents and you who have had the care of children know what it is to chasten without pity and yet at the same time discipline and punish with both love and pity. What do you do when you want your child to be the very finest example of manhood and character and citizenship? You pray for him and you love him so much that you would give the blood out of your veins for him—yet without pity you apply the rod of discipline and chastening.

It is actually pity that makes you punish him without pity!

That sounds like a beautiful mix-up, but that is the character and desire of our God for us if we are His children. It is the love and the pity of God for His children that prescribes the chastening of a cross so that we may become the kind of mature believers and disciples that He wants us to be.

I earnestly believe that God is trying to raise up a company of Christians in our day who are willing to be completely separated from all prejudices and all carnal desires. He wants those who are ready to put themselves at God's disposal, willing to bear any kind of cross—iron or lead or straw or gold or whatever—and to be the kinds of examples He needs on this earth.

The great question is: Is there a readiness, an eagerness among us for the kind of cross He wants to reveal through us?

Often we sing, "Hold Thou Thy cross before my closing eyes, Shine through the gloom and point me to the skies."

What a pathetic thing to see the cross so misunderstood in sections of Christianity. Think of poor souls who have never found the evangelical meaning and assurance of atonement and justification, cleansing and pardon. When they come to the time of death, the best they know is to clutch some manufactured cross to the breast, holding it tightly and hoping for some power to come from painted metal or carved wood to take them safely over the river.

No, no! That is not the kind of cross that helps. The cross that we want is that which will come to us from being in the will of God. It is not a cross on a hill nor a cross on a church. It is not the cross that can be worn around the neck. It must be the cross of obedience to the will of God, and we must embrace it, each believer for himself!

Willingness to suffer for Jesus' sake—this is what we have lost from the Christian church. We want our Easter to come without the necessity of a Good Friday. We forget that before the Redeemer could rise and sing among His brethren He must first bow His head and suffer among His brethren!

We forget so easily that in the spiritual life there must be the darkness of the night before there can be the radiance of the dawn. Before the life of resurrection can be known, there must be the death that ends the dominion of self. It is a serious but a blessed decision, this willingness to say, "I will follow Him no matter what the cost. I will take the cross no matter how it comes!"

Out of my own experience at this point I wrote a few words years ago which have long been my constant prayer:

"Oh God, let me die right, rather than letting me live wrong.

"Keep me, Lord, from ever hardening down into the state of being just another average Christian.

"Lord, I would rather reach a high point and turn off the light than to live a poor, useless life on a low level."

As individuals we often say that we want revival to come. Revival will come to us, and within us when we really want it, when we pay the price.

Have you come to the place of heart-searching, of travail in the Spirit, the place of blessed pain and trouble for Jesus' sake?

Without that decision and that commitment, you can pray on for revival to your dying day. You can join groups and stay up and pray for revival all night but exercise is all you will gain and sleep will probably be all you will lose!

We must dare to pray, "Oh God, crucify me from head to foot—I lay in dust life's glory dead!"

This is the reformation that we need!

Chapter Nine

Don't Throw Your Head Away—
You'll Need It!

"I am concerned about the attempts of some evangelicals to equate Christianity with all learning and all philosophy and all science!"

There is a great misunderstanding in Christianity today about the value of human effort and human ability in relation to the knowledge of God and fellowship with Him as His flock on this earth.

If you are longing after God with the expectation that you are going to be able to think your way through to Him, you are completely mistaken. This is a hunger that cannot be filled by human effort and our travail cannot be in the area either of our wits or our imagination, for in all of this there is an element of "unknowing," a deep, divine abyss of the Godhead. We dare not settle for anything less!

This is why I am concerned about the attempts being made by some evangelicals to equate Christianity with all learning and all philosophy and all science. If they continue on in their blind ways, they will find themselves ultimately in the camp of the theological liberals and under the cold frown of Almighty God.

Many of them apparently overlook the fact that the Spirit of God never promised to fill a man's head. The promise is that God will fill the heart, or man's innermost being. The Word of God makes it very plain that the church of Jesus Christ will never operate and minister and prosper by the stock of knowledge in the heads of Christian believers but by the warmth and urgency of God's love and compassion flowing through their beings.

Now, don't throw your head away—you are going to need it! I am convinced that God has made it plain that man alone, of all the creatures on earth, is created so that he can have fullness of knowledge about the earth and all the wonders and glories that it holds. I believe that through grace man can have a fullness of knowledge even about the works of God—but this certainly does not mean that we find Him and know Him and love Him through thought processes and human wisdom.

It is utterly and completely futile to try to think our way through to knowing God, Who is beyond our power of thought or visualization. This does not mean that it is impossible for us to think about Him—but it does mean that we cannot think around Him or think equal to Him or think up to Him!

This can be illustrated with one of the dangers of our times. A young man, for instance, has a hunger within himself for the knowledge of God and perhaps for the service of God. He goes to see a teacher who says, "Let's think this thing through." So the young man goes away saying, "Thank you, Doctor." He thinks he is all fixed up, but he hasn't received a thing. He has been taught in his head but his heart has not been satisfied, and he goes away still hungry.

If we are not in love with Christ Himself and if we are satisfied with a knowledge of the works of God and of systems of theology, our hunger for God will not be satisfied.

Now, I know that there is an intellectual element in the Gospel, for one of the attributes of deity is intellect. We call this element theology or doctrine. Human thought may engage theology, and it may engage doctrine. These things are necessary and right in their place, but there must be a seeking of the heart and being which is beyond the intellect.

An old hymn says, "The Spirit breathes upon the Word and brings the truth to light." How much more glory we discover in the scriptures when the Spirit breathes upon them. It is possible for the scriptures to be "taught" merely as an intellectual exposition, and if the Spirit is not allowed to breathe the life of God into the truth, our teaching can be useless and perhaps harmful.

When we sing, "Beyond the sacred page, I seek Thee, Lord," we do not mean that we are seeking contrary to or apart from the Word of God. The sacred page is not to be a substitute for God, although it has been made that by millions of people. The sacred page is not meant to be the end, but only the means toward the end, which is knowing God Himself.

In this current era many believers settle for knowing the text and having the text and arguing that because we have the text we must certainly have the experience.

The experience of God within the believer ought to result from the text, but it is possible to have the text and not have the experience!

This can be simply but plainly illustrated. Suppose a very rich man dies and leaves a will, the text of which passes on all of his millions to his only son. So the son and heir borrows the text of his father's will from the attorney and carries it around with him. He becomes ragged and hungry, begging on the street for a crust of bread.

But when someone says, "Poor fellow, you are in bad shape, weak and pale and sickly," the heir to the fortune reacts strongly.

"Don't talk to me like that," he says. "I have much more than I will ever be able to use!"

To prove it, he opens the will and reads: "Unto my dear son, Charles, I bequeath my property, my stocks and bonds, my bank accounts, my entire estate."

You see, Charles is completely satisfied with the text of the will. He has it and he holds it—but he has never had it executed, never had it filed for probate, never presented his legitimate claims to the inheritance. In actual experience, he has received nothing. He simply holds the text of the will.

In the same sense, a Christian may go around clutching the book of Ephesians and not realize that he is spiritually lean and hungry, pallid and weak, and ragged as well. If a pastor or an evangelist suggests that he could be in a more prosperous spiritual state, a strong, bristling reaction may result.

"Don't talk about me like that," he may say. "Am I not accepted in the Beloved? Do I not have everything in Jesus? Is not God my father and am I not an heir with God?"

How many of us does this portray, limping our ragged and lonely way down the street? It is one thing to have the text of the will—it is another thing to come into possession of the riches. The will of God is one thing but to have the will of God is another.

God has seen fit to give us a powerful Old Testament illustration of the necessity for a divine illumination, an experience of supernatural transformation and understanding in the quickening of the soul. It is in the account of the progress of Israel's high priest into the Holy of Holies. First in the order which God established was the Outer Court, over which there was no roof or covering. When the priest was there, he was aided by the natural light of the sun.

Then he passed through a veil into the Holy Place. Here there was no light of nature, but an artificial light was kept kindled by the priests themselves.

Still beyond was the Holy of Holies where there was neither natural light nor artificial light. There was only the Shekinah glory, the supernatural light of God shining from the mercy seat. When the priest came into the Holy of Holies, there was nothing human upon which he could lean. The intellect was of no consequence. There was no ecclesiastical light nor associate preacher in long tails intoning in a ministerial voice.

Think about that man chosen to minister as the high priest in those days. He came into the Holy of Holies knowing that the God who made heaven and earth was dwelling in fire between the wings of the cherubim. He knew that this was the great and living God with His thousands of attributes and His sea of endless and boundless Being. This man, a human, knew that God dwelt there and that as priest he was to move into that Presence.

In the Outer Court, there was the light above to help him. That could represent our church and denomination—the natural things upon which we often depend.

Moving into the Holy Place, there was still the artificial light, and perhaps that could be a representation of our theology.

But he had to go on until there was no natural or artificial light—only a supernatural shining! There in that Presence he had nothing to assure him but the character of God, nothing to protect him but the blood which he presented.

Furthermore, he was all alone. No other person could go in with the priest. His helpers could aid him in getting the veils apart, but then they had to back away with their eyes averted. Only the high priest with the blood could enter into that holiest place of all. Without the protection of the blood he would have burned as a leaf burns in fire. There was no human reassurance, no human help or counsel. There was no other human to pat him on the back, no one to show him the text, no one to help. He was all alone—but he had the character of God to assure him!

Brethren, when we finally have our meeting with God, it has to be alone in the depths of our being. We will be alone even if we are surrounded by a crowd. God has to cut every maverick out of the herd and brand him all alone. It isn't something that God can do for us en masse.

If it takes a crowd to get you converted, you have not been converted! If it takes a crowd to get you through to the fullness of the Holy Ghost, you are going to be disappointed.

I know that people do not want to be alone with God, but if your longing heart ever finds the living water, it will be alone. We humans want to help each other and that is good insofar as we can, but God wants us to press through to His Presence where there is no natural or artificial help. Our denominations have their place, but they cannot aid us at this point of aloneness. He asks that we come with a naked intent unto God. We must want God Himself —and nothing more!

When we present ourselves to Him in this way, what a blessing to have His assurance that God Himself has removed all of the legal hindrances to our access. It is a glorious hard core of fact that Jesus Christ has removed all of the legal hindrances!

There are many legal reasons why I should not go to heaven. There are governmental reasons why I should not go to heaven. I believe that a holy God must run His universe according to holy law—and I do not belong there because I have broken every one of those holy laws in some way. Therefore, there has to be a redemption, a justification of some kind if I am to have God and He is to have me.

Thank God, it has been done! The New Testament language is plain as can be—in Jesus Christ and through His death and resurrection every legal hindrance has been met and taken away. There is nothing to stop you except yourself—no reason why we cannot enter into all the depths of the fullness of God!

Here I must repeat—too many people are trying to think their way in. The only way to get in is to believe Him with our hearts forevermore, crying after Him and looking unto Him with a naked intent of love! The time comes when all we can do is believe God—believe what He says, believe Him and love Him!

The thinking process is not enough in this realm. The great God Almighty that fills the universe and overflows into immensity can never be surrounded by that little thing that we call our brain, our mind, our intellect—never, never, never! Never can we rise to face God by what we know and by what we are, but only by love and faith are we lifted thus to know Him and adore Him!

You know what a vacuum is—just an empty place where there isn't anything, not even air! They tell us that nature abhors a vacuum and unless the vacuum is surrounded by a hard casing of some kind, air or water or some other element will rush in and fill it. It should be happy knowledge to us that the kingdom of God also abhors a vacuum—and when you empty yourself, God Almighty rushes in!

Someone has written:

"Drawn by my Redeemer's love,
After Him I follow fast;
Drawn from earth to things above,
Drawn out of myself at last."

Drawn out of myself at last! If we are not able to make this confession, this becomes one of our greatest problems. If we have not been drawn from earth to things above, how can we be drawn out of ourselves to be spent in God? What a happy hour it becomes when we are drawn out of ourselves, and into that vacuum rushes the blessed Presence. Our subjection to Him is only because of our love for Him and our resignation to His will is for His pleasure alone, for He wills and merits to be thus loved and served!

The wonderful thing about the invitation of the Holy Spirit of God is that He doesn't say different things to different people. The Holy Spirit does not say two things—He says one thing! He says the same thing to all who are listening to Him.

He says, "Pour yourself out! Give yourself to Me! Empty yourself! Bring your empty earthen vessels! Come in meekness like a child!"

Drawn out of yourself by the Holy Spirit—for who knoweth the things of God but the Holy Spirit? Pulled out of the mud of your own ego, so that you have stopped thinking that you are somebody, at last you are delivered from yourself and are seeking God for Himself alone.

Think of that little woman centuries ago who pushed herself towards Jesus in the midst of a thronging crowd. Jesus was almost crushed in the crowd which pressed Him on every side. But one weak little woman completely ignored the pushing and the jostling, and as though she and the Saviour were alone, she touched the hem of His garment—and was healed!

Jesus turned His head and said, "Who touched me?" There were those around Him who answered, "That's a foolish question. You are in the middle of a mob, crowded and pushed and jostled and you ask, 'Who touched Me?'" But Jesus said, "I only asked who touched Me in faith? Who touched Me with love?" Many jostled Him—but this woman had really touched Him in faith and love and wonder—and she was made whole.

In our day there are still the crowds and the meetings and opportunities to reach out to Jesus in simple faith and love. But we have meetings where people revel in the crowd—and ignore the Lord. In the midst of our assemblies, isn't Jesus always waiting for someone to disregard the crowd and the circumstances and the traditions—and to push through in love and in faith to touch Him for His healing wholeness?

Oh, go back into the Word of God and consider

how thirsty the friends of God were for God Himself! The great difference between us and the Abrahams and the Davids and the Pauls is that they sought Him and found Him and seeking Him still, found Him and sought Him—continually!

We accept Him—and seek Him no more and that is the difference!

In the Song of Solomon in the Old Testament there is the appealing story of the girl who is very deeply in love with a young shepherd. She is so beautiful that a king is attracted to her and demands her favors, but she remains loyal to the simple shepherd, her love, who gathers lilies in the dew of the night and comes to seek her and call to her through the lattice. In many ways it is a picture of the Lord Jesus, the shepherd; His love and care for His bride, the Church; and the world represented by the king demanding or coaxing and trying to win our love.

In the scriptural account the shepherd calls, "Come, my beloved, rise up for the rain is over and gone and the singing of the birds is heard in the land."

But she turns him away with excuses about the ointment on her hands and that she has already retired for the night. So he goes away in sadness. However, she is condemned in her heart and rises from bed to go out and begin her search for her shepherd lover. When she is unable to find him, she is asked, "What is he above others that you are seeking him?"

"Oh, he is altogether lovely!" she replies. "He came and called for me. I heard him but didn't have the heart to go. Now I know what I have missed and I must find him."

At last she is able to confess, "I have found him

whom my soul loveth!" He had been grieved, but he was not far away. So it is with our Beloved—He is very near to us and He awaits our seeking!

Oh, a heart that is evermore crying after the One it loves is better indeed than the heart that has settled down to the little it already knows!

Chapter Ten

Forget That They Told You to Shut Up!

"Why do we not capture the divine illumination of Jesus Christ in our souls? Because there is a cloud of conceal-ment between us and the smiling face of God!"

I cannot help but believe that in our generation there is a great, concealing cloud over much of the fundamental, gospel church which has practically shut off our consciousness of the smiling face of God.

Textualism, a system of rigid adherence to words, has largely captured the church, with the language of the New Testament still being used but with the Spirit of the New Testament grieved.

The doctrine of verbal inspiration of the Scriptures, for instance, is still held, but in such a way that its illumination and life are gone and rigor mortis has set in. As a result religious yearning is choked down, religious imagination has been stultified and religious aspiration smothered.

The "hierarchy" and the "scribes" of this school of thought have told us and would teach us that we ought to shut up and quit talking about spiritual longing and desire in the Christian church.

We have already seen the reaction to this among the masses of evangelical Christians. There has been a revolt in two directions, a rather unconscious revolt, like the gasping of fish in a bowl where there is no oxygen. A great company of evangelicals has already gone over into the area of religious entertainment so that many gospel churches are tramping on the doorstep of the theater. Over against that, some serious segments of fundamental and evangelical thought have revolted into the position of evangelical rationalism which finds it a practical thing to make its peace with liberalism.

This is why the message of spiritual perfection and longing after God sounds so strange to our generation. On one side the masses proclaim, "I have accepted Jesus—whoop de doo! Let's go and have fun!" On the other, serious and reverent men are thinking their way perilously near to the borders of liberalism. Meanwhile, the New Testament message, objectives and methods are allowed to lie dormant, spurned and forgotten.

I have read for many years in the old devotional classics of the desire of the saints of God to keep the candles of their souls burning brightly, day by day. They sought to feel the divine fire in their hearts, to experience the blessedness of reconciliation with God. They are on record as always willing to renounce everything worldly in order to possess the treasure buried in the field of their hearts.

This is not new doctrine and it ought not to sound so different and strange to us. Has not Christ made full atonement for us, and should we not renounce everything that would keep us from the conscious experience of knowing and receiving the Kingdom of God within us?

God's face is turned toward us. The famed Lady Julian wrote long ago, "The precious amends our Lord hath made for man's sin have turned all our blame into endless honor!" Paul said it in this way, "Where sin abounds, grace does much more abound!"

It is glorious knowledge indeed that the smiling face of God is turned toward us. Why, then, do we not capture the wondrous, divine illumination of our Saviour, Jesus Christ? Why do we not know the divine fire in our own souls? Why do we not strive to sense and experience the knowledge and exhilaration of reconciliation with God?

Let me tell you why—it is because there is between us and the smiling face of God a cloud of concealment.

Some dismiss the subject by saying that it is all a matter of position with God—rather than possession! That is an answer as cold as dry ice and can only result in further coldness of soul.

I believe the smiling face of God is always turned toward us—but the cloud of concealment is of our own making.

The weather can be an illustration of these spiritual conditions which we allow and foster under a cloud. We are told that the sun is always shining somewhere. Since the day that God said, "Let the sun rule the day," the sun has continued to shine.

113

On earth, however, there are cloudy days, dark and misty days. I have seen the daytime so dark that the chickens had gone to roost and the lights had to be turned on.

Yes, the sun was shining on those dark days, shining just as brightly as on the clearest day in June. You don't need to worry about the sun—it will always shine! But the dark concealing cloud comes between the radiance of the sun and the earth.

Apply this to the Christian life. All that can be done for our salvation has been done. Christ has died for us and has been raised from the dead. The face of God shines down on us, but as Christians we allow the clouds of concealment to form.

Sometimes it may be a cloud caused by our stubborn pride. You may be a child of God, heaven is your home—and yet for a lifetime you may go on without the wondrous, divine illumination of the Saviour, Jesus Christ. You will not bend. You will yield neither to God nor man. Remember God's complaint against Israel. He said, "Your neck is brass and your forehead hard." He could not get Israel to bend, to yield to His will.

Self-will is a close relative of pride, and it will form a cloud that can hide the face of God. Actually, self-will can be a very religious thing for it can be accepted right into the church when you join. It can go right into the chamber with you when you pray. However, remember this—self-will is good-natured only when it can have its own way. Otherwise, it is grouchy and ill-tempered and cross. Under this cloud, we must examine ourselves and ask, "Is my surrender to God a complete surrender?"

Ambition can also bring the dark cloud of obscurity, and there is an ambition which operates in the area of religion. We claim things for ourselves—

perhaps some place or recognition which is not in the will of God, some advantage for ourselves. If it is something that we refuse to yield, insisting it is ours, and that we own it, it will bring that cloud of obscurity that nothing can penetrate. This is not just a word to laymen, for it can happen to ministers as well. The preacher ought not to be settled comfortably in his place with all of his ambitions getting priority. The preacher who is ambitious for himself will be found out. His pastorate, his preaching, his position—everything must be on the block and ready to be released if he is to know the smile and blessing of God!

Then there is the matter of presumption. Some Christians recognize that the cloud of concealment is there—so they presume that they can fast and pray and thus penetrate the cloud. But you cannot pray through this kind of cloud and fasting in such a case is just another kind of stubbornness.

We have no word from God indicating that long prayers will make everything right. In fact, there are Bible instances when God had to stop prayer meetings because they were useless!

You may recall that at one point in the history of Israel, the prophet Samuel was trying to pray for King Saul when God said, "Samuel, don't pray any more for Saul. He is through!"

In another instance Joshua was lying prone, his face down, and he was praying. We would have written a tract about his saintliness in prayer, but God said to him, "Joshua, what are you doing? I don't honor a man for complaining. Get up on your feet and deal with the situation in your crowd and then I will bless you!"

Genuine prayer is still the soul's sincere desire and God still answers. But we must give up this

115

idea that we can hang on to those things that bring the cloud and still be able to pray the cloud away. You cannot do it.

Think with me about fear. Fear is always the child of unbelief. Unfounded fears, linked with unbelief, become a cloud of obscurity over your head. You are afraid that you may become ill with cancer. You are afraid that your child may be crippled. You are afraid you will lose your job. You are afraid of Russia's guided missiles. The Lord wants us to surrender all of our fears to Him. He has made full provision for us—it is for us to surrender and trust. He is able!

Self-love will also form the cloud. Humans like to joke about it, but self-love is not a joking matter. A person who has been converted and is a Christian can still keep a cloud of concealment over him simply by loving himself. Self-love, self-admiration and gratification of self in a variety of ways—these are all self sins. The modern "scribe" excuses them and assures us that no one can do anything about them. Yet, what is this groan, this cry within us, that the candles of our souls might burn brightly and that we might know the divine illumination?

We must not forget that there is also a cloud that arises over our attitude towards money and possessions of all kinds. Money often comes between men and God. Someone has said that you can take two small ten-cent pieces, just two dimes, and shut out the view of a panoramic landscape. Go to the mountains and just hold two coins closely in front of your eyes—the mountains are still there but you cannot see them at all because there is a dime shutting off the vision of each eye. It is not so much a matter of great wealth and riches, however. It is a matter of attitude and whether or not the Lord is allowed to lead us and guide us in stewardship of much—or of little!

Have you checked out your attitudes about people, about society, about traditions? Are you determined that you are going to "fit in"? Are you spending most of your time trying to adjust and conform? Are you busy teaching your children that getting along with people is the most important part of life? If these are your goals, you will have a cloud over your heart, my Christian friend.

What is the answer to this growing list of cloud-forming attitudes? I think it is the willingness to put the cloud which is above us under our feet by faith and through grace!

Paul gave us this example when he said, "Forgetting those things which are behind and reaching forth unto those things which are before." He considered that those things which were behind him would have shut out the face of God if allowed to remain in the foreground. He put them under his feet by forgetting—defeats, mistakes, blunders, errors, rebukes.

This is the place of victory for the Christian – putting the cloud under our feet so that we see the smiling face of God again. The blessed thing is that He has been there all the time waiting for us to move up!

I had a vivid and memorable experience on an airplane leaving New York City some years ago. It was a dark, rainy afternoon and when we were aboard the plane, the relaxed, friendly pilot made a little speech about the miserable weather.

"We will be in the sunshine within 15 minutes after takeoff," he assured us. "The weather map shows that we will enjoy bright, clear weather all the way to Chicago after we get above the smog and the mist and the clouds."

As soon as we were in the air, the clouds became white under us and within a few moments we had put the clouds under our feet. The sun was shining brightly above and we flew those 900 miles in brilliant sunshine.

I didn't have to help that pilot at all, although I tried! I am the nervous type so I try to keep balancing the plane as we bank or turn. But that confident, smiling pilot doesn't have to count on my 159 pounds to balance that huge four-engine monster. He said he could get us up into the sunshine—and he did.

In the spiritual realm we have a Pilot who has promised us His sunlight, and if we will consent, He will put the clouds under our feet. He just asks that we be willing. If we let Him put the cloud beneath us, we find to our joy that He hides all of the past—all that has shamed and grieved and worried us! God waits for us to move upward into this place of spiritual restfulness and power.

"Into the sunshine in 15 minutes," the earthly pilot promised.

"Into the sunlight of God's will as soon as you are willing to put the clouds under your feet," our Heavenly Pilot promises us now!

You will discover a marvelous deliverance from bondage, a great freedom!

You will find a new delight and confidence in the Word of God!

You will experience a radiance and an illumination and a fragrance that you have never known before!

Our greatest need is to be willing—we need to act in faith.

Dr. A. B. Simpson wrote a hymn which is rarely sung now—for two reasons: The first is that the tune is hard to sing, and the second is that very few have the experience of which he wrote.

These are the words:

"I take the hand of love divine,
    I count each precious promise mine
  With this eternal countersign—
    I take—He undertakes!

"I take Thee, Blessed Lord,
    I give myself to Thee;
  And Thou, according to Thy Word,
    Do'st undertake for me!"

This is the basic question for each of us—will we take from the hand of God all that He has provided? He has already undertaken for us. Will we "take the hand of love divine" and "claim each precious promise mine"?

Brethren, God waits for your faith and your love, and He doesn't ask whose interpretation of Scripture you have accepted. The New Testament tells of believers who met and prayed together, the strong taking the burdens of the weak, and all praying for those who had fallen. The place was shaken, and they were all filled with the Holy Ghost.

"Pay no attention to that," we have been told by "interpreters." "That is not for us." So it has been ruled out by interpretation and the blessed Dove has been forced to fold His wings and be silent.

Our hearts tell us that these modern scribes who are long on interpretation are wrong in spirit. Our own longing souls tell us that the old saints and hymn writers and the devotional giants were right!

Years ago Paul Rader preached a powerful sermon on the theme that "out of man's innermost being shall flow rivers of living water." Later, two men who had heard the sermon asked Mr. Rader to meet with them for a meal and for discussion. One man began by saying, "Mr. Rader, you preached a good sermon, but you are all wrong dispensationally." The other added, "Mr. Rader, you are a good preacher and a good brother—the problem is that you have the wrong interpretation."

I understand that Mr. Rader did not answer. They bowed their heads to pray before eating their meal, and when Mr. Rader finally looked across the table at the first brother, he saw that something had happened. Tears were streaming down the man's face, and his shoulders shook with emotion. Finally he was able to say, "Brother Rader, we have the interpretation, but you have the rivers of blessing!"

Some are going to continue to plod along with dryness—sticking to interpretation! But some of us want God's blessing and God's stirring and God's best for our lives at any cost! We have the Saviour's Word that the Holy Spirit has come to us in our present world. He is mine and He is yours, our sweet possession!

No man can set up the rules as to how much you can have of God. The Lord Himself has promised that as far as He is concerned He is willing to keep the candles of your soul brightly burning!

Chapter Eleven

Caution: Self-Will
Will Scratch Your Back!

*"If it were true that the Lord puts the Christian believer
on the shelf every time he fails or does something wrong,
I would have been a piece of statuary by this time!"*

Man's very human habit of trusting in himself is
generally the last great obstacle blocking his pathway to victory in Christian experience.

Even the Apostle Paul, writing in his New Testament letters, confessed that his confidence in God
was in completely opposite ratio to his confidence in
himself. Paul made it very plain that it was only
after giving up the last inclination to trust in himself

that he became immersed in the sufficiency of Christ.

We can learn much from the experiences of Paul and the humility of his testimony, "I know that in me dwelleth no good thing." He had discovered that to be fully surrendered to God and the will of God meant that first he must come to an entire and radical distrust of himself.

After he became willing to look within his own being, Paul had no further confidence in himself and couldn't say enough against himself. But when he went forth before men in the compulsion of ministry for Christ, he seemed to stand sure with a great cosmic confidence because he had met God and could honestly declare that "we have this treasure in earthen vessels that the excellency of the power may be of God and not of us."

Paul was being continually thrown into spiritual combat as he moved forward in his declaration of Jesus as Christ and Lord. He knew the blessing and the power of operating from a position of strength —the fact that he held no illusions about himself and depended completely upon the Spirit of God.

"I am nothing except for the grace of God," he said.

"I am the least of the apostles and not worthy to be called an apostle," he wrote.

"Christ Jesus came into the world to save sinners of whom I am chief," he acknowledged.

This all adds up to a startling statement of truth held not only by Paul but by all of the great saints who have done exploits for God. They would all remind us that those who insist on trusting human self will never obtain the desired victory in spiritual combat, for they will presume vainly in their own strength!

To become effective men of God, then, we must

know and acknowledge that every grace and every virtue proceeds from God alone, and that not even a good thought can come from us except it be of Him.

I think that most of us can glibly quote the scriptures about the lessons that Paul learned without actually coming to this place of complete distrust of ourselves and our own strengths. Our self-trust is such a subtle thing that it still comes around whispering to us even after we are sure it is gone.

In our search for God and for victory, perhaps we have put away all the sins that have plagued us. We have tried to deal with all of the self sins that we know, allowing them to be crucified. At this point we have stopped boasting, and we are sure that we have stopped loving ourselves. It may be that in the process we have humbled ourselves and publicly gone forward to an altar to confess our need and to pray.

Now, this is my caution—after we have humbled ourselves there is a possibility that our subtle self-trust may prove to be stronger than ever, for it has a better foundation upon which to build! After we have put away our sins and given up our will and after we have taken a position of confession and humility, our self-trust is quick to whisper its consolation deep within us. Often when this has happened, Christians have made the mistake of believing that this whisper of consolation comes from the Holy Ghost—and that is why we are so weak when we think we are strong!

Just what is the whisper that is likely to come to us deep within our being?

"You have really come a long way, and you have advanced far ahead of others," self-trust is likely to whisper. "You have put sin behind you, and you have humbled yourself. You will be a power for you are not one of the dead ones. You may trust yourself now because you have left much behind, and parted with friends, and paid a price! You are really getting somewhere. You will have victory now —with God's help, of course!"

I call this a kind of back-scratching—and our old self knows just when to come through with it because it feels so good to us in terms of consolation and comfort. It is the process of reverting right back to self-trust, and almost all of the joy that the average Christian knows is the back-scratching that self gives him.

When self whispers an assurance to you that you are different—look out! "You are different," self whispers, and then adds the proof. "You have given up enough things to make you a separated Christian. You love the old hymns, and you can't stand the modern nonsense. You have a good standard—none of those movies and none of this modern stuff for you!"

You don't really know what is happening to you, but you are feeling pretty good about everything by this time. But the good feeling is strictly from being coddled and comforted and scratched by a self that has refused to die. Self-trust is still there— and you thought it had gone!

Now, what is our great encouragement in view of all that we know about ourselves? It is the fact that God loves us without measure, and He is so keenly interested in our spiritual growth and progress that He stands by in faithfulness to teach and instruct and discipline us as His dear children!

I once wrote something about how God loves us and how dear we are to Him. I wasn't sure I should put it down on paper, but God knew what I meant.

I said, "The only eccentricity that I can discover in the heart of God is that a God such as He is should love sinners such as we are!" God has that strange eccentricity but it still does not answer our wondering question, "Why did God love us?"

On this earth a mother will love the boy who has betrayed her and sinned and is now on his way to life in prison. That seems to be a natural thing for a mother, but there is nothing natural about this love of God. It is a divine thing—it is forced out by the inward pressure within the heart of God. That is why He waits for us, puts up with us, desires to lead us on—He loves us!

You can put all of your confidence in God. He is not angry with you, His dear child! He is not waiting to pounce on you in judgment—He knows that we are dust and He is loving and patient towards us.

If it were true that the Lord would put the Christian on the shelf every time he failed and blundered and did something wrong, I would have been a piece of statuary by this time! I know God and He isn't that kind of God. He will bring judgment when judgment is necessary, but the scriptures say that judgment is God's strange work. Where there is a lifetime of rebellion, hardened unbelief, love of sin and flagrant refusal of His love and grace, judgment will fall. But with His dear children, God watches over us for spiritual growth and maturity, trying to teach us how necessary it is for us to trust in Him completely and to come to a complete distrust of ourselves.

There are at least three ways that God may use to teach us this necessity of completely distrusting ourselves.

Occasionally this lesson from God has come by

holy inspiration. I suppose the best and easiest way to find out that you are no good is to have God flash that knowledge suddenly into your soul. I know that it has happened to some people. I think of the writings of the saintly Brother Lawrence who testified that God gave him this vision and knowledge of himself in such a way that for years he was never out of the conscious presence of God!

"When I took the cross and decided to obey Jesus and walk in His holy way, I knew that I might be called upon to suffer," Brother Lawrence wrote. "But, for some reason, God never counted me worthy of much suffering. He just let me continue to trust in Him completely after I put all my self-trust away. It is a life of carrying His cross and believing that He is in me and around me and near me, and praying without ceasing."

Lady Julian, also, wrote in her book of the gracious experience when God, by holy inspiration, gave light to her heart so that she realized instantly that she was worthless in herself and that Jesus Christ was everything!

At this point someone is sure to say, "But Mr. Tozer, I already know that I am bad. I am a believer in total depravity!"

My reply is this: it is possible to be a confirmed believer in total depravity and still be as proud as Lucifer! It is possible to believe in depravity and still trust in yourself in such a way that the face of God is hidden and you are kept from victory.

We are dealing with something else here—not theological total depravity. We may not understand how we can inherit evil from our fathers, but there is no argument with the fact that as soon as we are big enough to sin, we go directly into the business of sinning. It has been true of every child of every race and of every nationality—we are born bad, and in that sense we are all alike.

The lesson that we are trying to draw here is the necessity of God revealing by the Holy Spirit the utter weakness of the child of God who is still putting trust in himself. A teacher can tell you that you are weak and that all of your righteousnesses are but filthy rags and you may still go through school and get a long degree and go out proudly to be a missionary or a preacher or a Bible teacher. Our selfish condition—if we are still trusting in ourselves—can only be demonstrated to us by the Holy Spirit. When the knowledge comes and we lean only on Him, we will know that "conscious presence" in which Brother Lawrence lived and rejoiced continually day by day!

Another way in which we may have to learn this lesson from God is with harsh scourgings. Perhaps this makes me appear to belong to the seventeenth century for it does not have a popular sound in our day. We are more likely to bring in the cow bells and try to give everyone a little bit of pleasure than to faithfully declare that our dear heavenly Father may use harsh scourging to teach His children distrust of self.

Actually, I would prefer to preach from the twenty-third Psalm every Sunday for a year. Then I would take up the fifty-third chapter of Isaiah and after a long time I would come to the thirteenth chapter of First Corinthians.

But if I should do that, what would happen to my congregation in the meantime? The flock of God would become the softest, sweetest and spongiest group of no-goods that ever came together!

The Lord does have to give us chastening and discipline and harsh scourgings at times. None of you would feed your children continually on a diet of sugar cookies—they would lose their teeth! There must be a diet with solid stuff if they are to be vigorous and well.

We speak of harsh scourgings and immediately we think of that man Job in the Old Testament. We have a great deal of pity for Job and in human sympathy many people take Job's part against God—and certainly against his wife! But have you ever noticed that Job was far from being humble, even though he was a praying man and one who made sacrifices because his children might have sinned at their party the night before. But we finally hear him saying in that long discourse, "Oh, that I were as in months past, as in the days when God preserved me . . . when I went out to the gate through the city, when I prepared my seat in the street."

He was a "big shot," you know, and that is what they did then. They had a place at the head of the street where the honored men were seated.

"When the young men saw me," he said, "they hid themselves; and the aged arose and stood up."

Who is this coming down the street? The honorable Mister Job!

"Oh, here I am now, lying in this ash pile," he said. "They have cast me out. No one would vote for me now, but there was a day when princes refrained from talking in my presence and laid their hands on their mouths."

Brother Job was no ordinary rag picker—he was a great man! But he knew it—and that was the trouble and that's why those harsh things happened to him. If you are great and you happen to suspect it, and you are God's child—things will start happening to you, too.

Finally, seeing God's majesty and power, Job

said, "Oh God, I have been talking and talking and talking, but now I put my hand over my mouth—I am vile!" It was only then that the Lord could say to him, "All right, Job, now pray for the rest of them." So Job prayed for those who had tried to comfort him, and God gave back to him twice as much as he had possessed previously.

There is a third way, also, in which God may be trying to deal with our weakness of self-trust. We are familiar with this method if we study the Bible, for it is the discipline of manifold temptations.

Some Christians are prone to sink into discouragement when called upon to face temptations, but I think that these disciplines should become a spiritual encouragement to us. God does not allow the temptations and testings to come to us because He is trying to show us up—He is dealing with us through this means because we are Christians, we are His children! He is dealing with us in the midst of temptations because He has found our conscience is tender enough to listen and because we are willing to be drawn closer to Him. He is only trying to teach us this necessary lesson of distrust of self.

When temptations come, you are not to throw in the towel and say, "Oh God, I guess this proves that you don't want me!" Instead, it should be a sign to you as you come through the testing by His grace that you are nearer your eternal home today than you were yesterday!

There are scriptural examples of men of God who were sifted in the course of such testing experiences. Think of blustery Peter and his denial of the Saviour when wicked men arrested Jesus and put Him through the mockery of a trial before taking Him out to Calvary to be crucified. What if Peter had taken his own actions as proof that he was not really a Christian disciple? It was a difficult course, but it was a most powerful lesson from the heavenly Father, revealing to Peter what an ineffective believer he would be if he continued to trust in his own strength.

None of us can really tell how weak and useless we are until God has exposed us—and no one wants to be exposed! But God knows so much better than we do that He must expose us for our own good.

Neither do any of us really know how unstable we are until we have been exposed by the Holy Ghost. Peter was a big, bold, strong fisherman, and it seemed easy for him to say to the Lord, "Let everyone else run away, but I will always stand by. You can count on me, Master!" I am sure it was hard for him to take the answer that Jesus gave him: "Before the rooster crows tonight you will say three times that you do not know me!" But Jesus knew the instability of the man who still tried to stand in his own strength and in his own self-trust.

We do not really know how unstable we are, and we often refuse to admit the truth when we find out, when we are exposed. That is why it is too dangerous to trust our good habits and our virtues— and that is why our distrust of ourselves must be the work of God's hand!

Oh, brethren, He is our God, and this is my advice —love Him and trust Him and depend only upon Him! If we insist upon trusting ourselves, our training, our education, our talents and our human judgment—we make God less than He is and we make man more than he is! We take the glory from God and give it to our converted and sanctified self—and that is shameful, because it takes from God the ultimate and final trust. Even when we say that we know that God is the source and the fountain of all things, and we recite His attributes and become expert in theology, we may still believe in our hearts that we are more than we really are!

This is where we need repentance and forgiveness. I recall that Brother Lawrence, writing about the pattern of victory in the daily walk with God, gave a simple and direct solution to failures and wrong-doing. He advised that if we ever make a slip and do that which is wrong, we should not ignore it and let it remain unconfessed and unforgiven.

"I would go straight to the Lord and say, 'Now Lord, that's me—and if you don't forgive me and help me, that's what you can expect for that's me!'" is what he wrote in essence. "God forgave me, and I went right on from there."

Some people insist that repentance and forgiveness must be a long, drawn-out affair, but I don't agree that it must necessarily be so. I believe the best repentance is turning to God and away from our sin—and not doing it any longer!

That is the best repentance in the whole, wide world. Why does it take us so long to put our complete trust in God when He has made it so simple and so rewarding to yield what we are to Him!

Chapter Twelve

How Long Can You Slight
the Christ of God?

*"How long should it take us to yield completely to
this One who has been made both Lord and Christ—yet
loves us with an everlasting love?"*

Have you ever heard one of our modern, Christian
activists say, "I am still busy looking around for
the best doctrine on holiness," or "I don't know
when I will find a doctrine of the deeper life that
is satisfactory to me!"

There is really only one answer to this kind of

a quest—turn your eyes upon Jesus and commit yourself fully and completely to Him because He is God and Christ, Redeemer and Lord, "The same yesterday, today and forever!"

In these matters of spiritual blessing and victory, we are not dealing with doctrines—we are dealing with the Lord of all doctrine! We are dealing with a Person who is the Resurrection and the Life and the Source from whom flows all doctrine and all truth.

How can we be so ignorant and so dull that we try to find our spiritual answers and the abounding life by looking beyond the only One who has promised that He would never change? How can we so readily slight the Christ of God who has limitless authority throughout the universe? How long should it take us to yield completely and without reservation to this One who has been made both Lord and Christ— and yet continues to be the very same Jesus who still loves us with an everlasting love?

I never want to come to a halt, pleading that I hold the right and proper doctrines—because I know that the only righteousness I can ever possess is His righteousness imparted to me. I claim nothing and my testimony is the same as Martin Luther's prayer: "Oh, Lord Jesus, Thou art my righteousness —I am Thy sin!"

The only sin Jesus had was mine, Luther's and yours—and the only righteousness we can ever have is His.

It seems to be very hard for us to comprehend the importance of the fact that Christ does not change and that there is no fluctuation in His character, in His nature, in His resources, in His love and mercy.

Because change is everywhere around us at all times on this earth and among human beings, it is difficult for us to grasp the eternal and unchanging nature and person of Jesus Christ. We are well aware that if we elevate a man, giving him a high position with great influence and plenty of money—he is going to change! He may not realize it and often he will deny it, but he is not going to be the same in character and attitude and habits and manner of life. He will become proud—and probably aloof and unsympathetic! He will probably have his nose up in the air and it will be hard for him to recognize his old friends.

But nothing about our Lord Jesus Christ has changed down to this very hour. His love has not changed. It hasn't cooled off, and it needs no increase because He has already loved us with infinite love and there is no way that infinitude can be increased. His compassionate understanding of us has not changed. His interest in us and His purposes for us have not changed.

He is Jesus Christ, our Lord. He is the very same Jesus. Even though He has been raised from the dead and seated at the right hand of the Majesty in the heavens, and made Head over all things to the Church, His love for us remains unchanged. Even though He has been given all authority and power in heaven and in earth, He is the very same Jesus in every detail. He is the same yesterday, today and forever!

It is hard for us to accept the majestic simplicity of this constant, wonder-working Jesus. We are used to getting things changed so that they are always bigger and better!

An important man in the Old Testament represents all of us in our humanity. He was afflicted with leprosy and he wanted the prophet of God to come and strike a noble pose and in a very dignified and proper way say to the leprosy, "Be gone!" But the prophet said he should take his pride in hand and go to the Jordan river and bathe in the waters of the Jordan in order to be healed. In other words, God asked him to do something very simple.

You and I are not always satisfied with the manner in which God deals with us. We would very much like to do something new, something different, something big and dramatic—but we are called back. For everything we need, we are called back to the simplicity of the faith, to the simplicity of Jesus Christ and His unchanging person.

The very same Jesus—a Brother who bears your image at the right hand of the Father, and who knows all your troubles and your weaknesses and sins, and loves you in spite of everything!

The very same Jesus—a Saviour and Advocate who stands before the Father taking full responsibility for you and being easier to get along with than the nicest preacher you ever knew and being easier to approach than the humblest friend you ever had.

The very same Jesus—He is the sun that shines upon us, He is the star of our night. He is the giver of our life and the rock of our hope. He is our safety and our future. He is our righteousness, our sanctification, our inheritance. You find that He is all of this in the instant that you move your heart towards Him in faith. This is the journey to Jesus that must be made in the depths of the heart and being. This is a journey where feet do not count.

Many of our Christians are activists—they are good at footwork and they are engaged in many religious journeys, but they do not seem to move up any closer to Jesus in heart and in spirit. This modern religious emphasis on activity reminds me of the Japanese mice that I have seen in the windows of the pet store. Don't stop and look at them if you are the nervous type. I do not know why they call them dancing mice because they don't waltz—they just run continually. I think they must be fundamentalists, brethren—they are on the go all the time! Some Christians seem to feel that it is a mark of spirituality to attend banquets and seminars and workshops and conferences and courses, night after night, week after week.

This naturally brings up some lessons from the New Testament record concerning the sisters, Martha and Mary. I think it was plain that Martha loved Jesus but her concept of devotion was activity. She was an active girl and she believed that because she loved the Lord, she ought to be doing something all the time to show it. Mary also loved the Lord Jesus but with a different attitude in her devotion. She was fervently occupied in spirit about the love of His Godhead! Our Lord knew the difference then and He knows the difference today.

Actually, our craze for activity brings few enriching benefits into our Christian circles. If you look into our churches, you will find groups of half-saved, half-sanctified, carnal people who know more about social niceties than they do about the New Testament; and more about love stories and soap operas than they do about the Holy Spirit.

When they get together, they have no trouble in thinking up things to do, but there is a question in my mind as to whether all of these things ought to be done in the name of the Lord!

It is not enough just to be rushing somewhere to another meeting, another discussion, another dialogue. Jesus commended Mary for knowing the value of the one thing that is necessary—that God should be loved and praised above all other business which may occupy us bodily or spiritually. Mary was fervently occupied in spirit about the love of His Godhead. I like that—although I know it sounds strange and almost heretical to our modern activists.

My plea is that we will not be satisfied to continue on as "external" Christians. The extroverted Christian lives largely for the externals of Christianity, and therefore sadly neglects his inner life and growth.

Recall what happened when Jesus said to the disciples, "Go ye into all the world and preach the gospel to every creature!"

Peter jumped up right away, grabbed his hat and would have been on his way, but Jesus stopped him, and said, "Not yet, Peter! Don't go like that. Tarry until you are endued with power from on high, and then go!"

I believe that our Lord wants us to learn more of Him in worship before we become busy for Him. He wants us to have a gift of the Spirit, an inner experience of the heart, as our first service, and out of that will grow the profound and deep and divine activities which are necessary.

Years ago I heard Dr. Oliver Buswell warn that our evangelical churches were beginning to suffer from what he called "a rash of amateurism." He didn't know what a prophet he was—for now we have religious amateurs running in all directions!

The first thing we tell our young converts, the babes in Christ, is, "Here is a handful of tracts—now get out and get busy!"

But the Lord did not say that. He spoke about the first thing that was needful—to be fervently occupied in spirit with the love of Christ's Godhead, and to love and praise Him above all other business, bodily or spiritual. That's what it means to love God, to be a spiritual person—to have an ordained and measured affection plainly directed unto God Himself! This is more than a flash of spiritual feeling or emotion—it doesn't necessarily have anything to do with goose-pimples!

An ordained and measured pouring out of our love and affection—and this cannot be done without some involvement of the emotions. But it is not like a rainy day when a cloudburst may pour itself out in a few hours—and then there may be a dry spell for weeks. It is a demonstrated love for the Lord Jesus Christ, continually pouring itself out, ordained and measured!

Knowing and loving the unchanging Christ with this kind of adoration will keep us from falling into a number of subtle traps which have long plagued unstable believers.

It will keep us from stumbling over "people." You will continue to have your longing after God, but you will no longer stumble over the imperfections of men and women around you. It was Thomas à Kempis who wrote in *The Imitation of Christ*: "If thou would'st have peace of heart, do not inquire too earnestly into other men's matters." If you spend time examining your Christian brother, you will find him lacking in some things. Don't forget that all idols have feet of clay.

We have plain teaching that the Lord does not want His children to become "saint-worshippers." He doesn't want you to become a preacher-worshipper or a teacher-worshipper. God wants to deliver you from the best man you know so that man can die and be removed and you won't backslide!

Another thing we know is that this kind of love and devotion will keep you from stumbling over the praises of people. I am of the opinion that perhaps the praises people try to give us are more dangerous to our Christian walk than their blame.

The devil wants us to believe that we are saintly and superior to other Christians—that's the way he hooks us! That's why he gets other people to tell us how well we are doing—and how we are passing right by other Christians who are not humble and warm-hearted "like we are!"

Every time you take a new step forward for God the devil will have some means of communicating to you the fact that God is proud of you—and that you are wonderful! As soon as he can get you interested enough to say, "Yes, I guess that's true," you have had it, brother!

Now, what about the blame we often get from our fellow Christians? Are you hidden away in Christ Himself and so occupied in spirit that you take little heed of what men do or say about you?

I have observed that as long as we sit frozen to our chair, making no spiritual progress, no one will bother us. No one will come and put an arm around our shoulder and urge us: "Thou hast dwelt in this mount long enough—rise therefore and go across this Jordan!"

But, if we start to cross Jordan urged on by our own spiritual thirst and desire, at least fourteen people will ask prayer for us in the concern that we are losing our minds.

During my ministry I have seldom been blamed for being cold when I was cold. People don't come to the pastor and say, "You are no longer warm-hearted—what has happened to your spiritual life?"

I have concluded that you can be backslidden, and in the rank and file of evangelical Christians no one will take any notice of it. There will be no rebuke.

On the other hand, they will jump down your throat and accuse you of showing off as soon as you start to seek God in earnest for victory and blessing! It does seem odd that we can be in the Christian faith and yet we are going to have bleeding fingernails and sore knees for every inch of ground that we take away from the devil!

That's why so many Christians are taking so little! Many of us had actually taken more spiritual ground when we were converted than we now possess.

I picked up a little piece of printed paper on a muddy road in West Virginia many years ago. I will never know who put it there, but I know God planned that I should see it and remember it.

There was only one paragraph and it said, "There are only two things known in this universe that are bigger when they were born than when they get their growth. One is a wasp and the other is a church member."

I don't know about the wasp, but I do know that many church members start out with a blaze, and then they look around and decide that they should be more like other Christians—just settled down. Soon they are as backslidden as the rest. The amazing thing is that so many people can be so backslidden and never know it!

What a sad condition for Christians who are in the church of the mighty Redeemer and Deliverer who is eternally the Victor, the Rock of Ages. Why can't we claim all that He has promised for us?

In view of much of today's dispensational teaching about Bible interpretation, the apostles, miracles of God, and the fullness of the Spirit, I must remind you that the Lord Jesus Christ is the same yesterday, today and forever. That allows me to tell you something blessed and heartening which I have found to be true, and which I will stand by to the end of time.

This is my finding: there is nothing that Jesus has ever done for any of His disciples that He will not do for any other of His disciples!

Where did the "dividers-of-the-Word-of-Truth" get their teaching that all the gifts of the Spirit ended when the last apostle died? They have never furnished chapter and verse for that. When some men beat the cover off their Bible to demonstrate how they stand by the Word of God, they should be reminded that they are only standing by their own interpretation of the Word.

I find nothing in the Bible that says the Lord has changed. He has the same love, the same grace, the same mercy, the same power, the same desires for the blessing of His children. You will have to prove it to me if you take the position that Jesus Christ refuses to do for you something that He did for any other of His disciples! He is just the same toward everyone and everything.

His attitude toward the proud is unchanged. In the Bible record the proud men who came to Jesus got uniform treatment. Somehow, they were never able to discover that side of Jesus which is gentle and loving, kind and merciful. The proud always came up on the wrong side of Jesus, and they got that which the proud will always get from Jesus— justice and judgment, rebuke, warning and woe! It was the same with the self-righteous, the insincere, the hypocrites—they all came up on the wrong side of Jesus!

It is about time that the modern artists who paint pictures of Jesus should be told that He was not a pretty, curly-haired weakling. They should be told the truth—that He is the Christ of God and He will

141

come riding through the skies on a white horse and with a sword at His side. He will judge the world, He will call all men to their feet and they will honor Him for His majesty, His glory, His power, His purity, and for creation itself.

He is the same Jesus—He will always be the same!

He is always the same to the meek, the mourner, the brokenhearted, the penitent sinner. His attitude is always the same towards those who love Him, the honest-hearted person. These are the people who come up to Jesus on the right side—and He never turns them away. He is ready with forgiveness. He is ready with comfort. He is ready with blessing.

We cannot understand this readiness of Jesus to love us and help us and bless us—because He does not really need us. One of His attributes is omnipotence—so He doesn't need us. But the secret is this —He loves us!

Think of a man who is president of a great, thriving corporation. He has cars and airplanes at his disposal and hundreds of people who will carry out his orders immediately. This great man has a three-year-old daughter. Does he need her? No, of course not, but he loves her and he wants her! His heart is responsive to her needs and desires.

So it is with us. Before we were born, God was God, the Lord God Almighty! He has never needed us. None of our human talents and abilities are significant to Him. But He needs our love and wants our love!

The Apostle John leaned his ear against the beating heart of the Son of God and the Lord recognized His love and devotion and called him "the disciple whom Jesus loved." He loved the rest of the dis-

142

ciples, too, but He couldn't love them as much because they didn't reciprocate as much.

Jesus is still just the same towards those who seek His fellowship. He wants to be with those who are occupied with the love of His Godhead! Our relationship with Him is all summed up in this simple fact—everything you need is found in Jesus Christ, the Son of God!

He is God and He is the Son of Man. He is all the guilty sinner needs and He is more than the fondest expectation of the loftiest saint. We can never go beyond Him. We can never learn all that He is able to teach. We can never use all of the spiritual power and victory He is able to provide.

It is good for us to remember how strong He is—and how weak we are. I settled this issue a long time ago. I tell you I have talked to God more than I have talked to anyone else. I have reasoned more with God and had longer conferences with God than with anybody else.

And what did I tell Him? Among other things, I told Him, "Now, Lord, if I do the things I know I should do, and if I say what I know in my heart I should say, I will be in trouble with people and with groups—there is no other way!

"Not only will I be in trouble for taking my stand in faith and honesty, but I will certainly be in a situation where I will be seriously tempted of the devil!"

Then, after praying more and talking to the Lord, I have said, "Almighty Lord, I accept this with my eyes open! I know the facts and I know what may happen, but I accept it. I will not run. I will not hide. I will not crawl under a rug. I will dare to stand up and fight because I am on your side—and I know that when I am weak, then I am strong!"

So I don't let anyone praise me and I try not to pay attention to those who would blame me; I find that this is not difficult, for I am only a servant of the holiest man that ever walked the streets of Jerusalem—and they called Him a devil!

This is how I have learned to stand fast for Christ, and all that He is to His own!